the aside of "vignettes," the dramatic delivery of "focal points," and a final secret unveiled. And in her tales I would find the same—a seemingly leisurely delivery would lull me into a complacent enjoyment and then suddenly I'd be faced with a moral. Emily is not just a poet and a gardener. I suspect she would have made a good trial lawyer.

So here I present to you Emily Whaley and her stories. Stories about gardens. Stories about how to garden—and how to serve a meal and teach somebody to dance. There's a chap-

ter on each of her parents and one on Charleston preservation and tourism and another on a Russian spy. This is a real book. A real how-to guide for life — the kind of simple and exciting life where giving and taking are mixed up together and joy and laughter are just a turn in the path away.

Wait. Before closing I should say it's impossible not to fall in love with Emily. But I must admit to you that I never felt quite comfortable enough to call her Cheeka, as she insists you must. She's still Emily to me. And I was one of those rare ones she couldn't teach to dance. But she fed me well — lunches just like my own Pinopolis-raised grandmother used to fix. And she did her level best to explain gardening and she treated me royally. And yes, what follows is thoroughly hers. My job here has consisted of transcribing, retyping, and pruning — she's a strong advocate of pruning. Anyway, this is Emily Whaley — warm, funny, earthy, and oh, so opinionated. She changed my life for the better. Let her do the same for you.

Mrs. Whaley and Her Charleston Garden

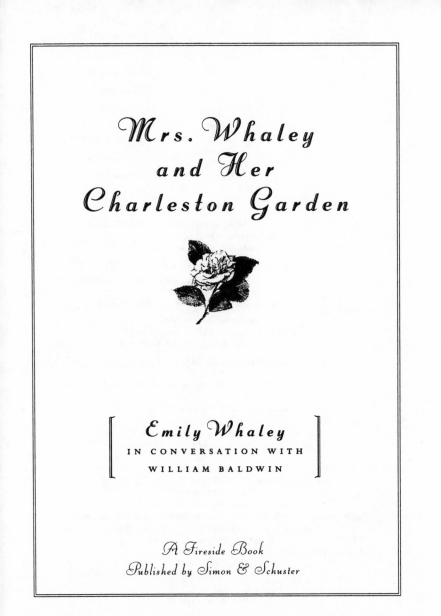

Emily Whaley
IN CONVERSATION WITH
WILLIAM BALDWIN

A Fireside Book
Published by Simon & Schuster

F

FIRESIDE
Rockefeller Center
1230 Avenue of the Americas
New York, NY 10020

Copyright © 1997 by Emily Whaley and William Baldwin

All rights reserved,
including the right of reproduction
in whole or in part in any form.

Published by arrangement with Algonquin Books of Chapel Hill

First Fireside Edition 1998

FIRESIDE and colophon are registered trademarks of Simon & Schuster Inc.

Illustrations by Charles DeAntonio
Blueprints on pages 18–19 by Loutrel Briggs
Designed by Louise Fili, Mary Jane Callister/Louise Fili Ltd

Manufactured in the United States of America

3   5   7   9   10   8   6   4   2

Library of Congress Cataloging-in-Publication Data
Whaley, Emily.
Mrs. Whaley and her Charleston garden/Emily Whaley; in
conversation with William Baldwin.—1st Fireside ed.
p.   cm.
"A Fireside Book."
Originally published: 1st ed. Chapel Hill, N.C.: Algonquin Books
of Chapel Hill, 1997.
1. Whaley, Emily.   2. Gardeners—South Carolina—Charleston—
Biography.   3. Whaley, Emily—Homes and haunts—South Carolina—
Charleston.   4. Gardening—South Carolina—Charleston.
I. Baldwin, William P.   II. Title.
[SB63.W46A3   1998]
635'.092—dc21

[B]   97-46661

CIP
ISBN 0-684-84387-0

To all the present and future
gardeners in my family

Contents

Introduction

by William Baldwin

INSERTING MYSELF LIKE THIS BETWEEN THE READER AND EMILY WHALEY IS A BIT like stepping in front of a speeding automobile. Emily's tan Volvo station wagon to be exact. Yes, she is definitely a high-energy person. As you'll soon discover, she's got "an opinion on everything." Not just gardening. Everything. And she has not just the courage of her convictions but the wit and boundless enthusiasm to back them up. Let me put it another way. On the outside Emily Whaley is eighty-five years old and moves with the imperial bearing of a grand Southern matron. But on the inside she's a knobby-kneed fourteen-year-old country girl bouncing across a homemade tennis court.

Charleston, South Carolina, where she lives, is a city of gardens and gardeners. When you drive over the high camel hump of the Cooper River bridge (which she likes to do for fun), you look down on red tin roofs and amazing expanses of greenery. Each fall the city hosts a garden festival and each spring even more visitors return to enjoy Southern gardens at their best. And every year two or three thousand of these visitors pass through Emily's Church Street garden. She and the garden are already well known. The *New York Times* sends reporters to interview her. *Southern Accents* did a layout. Practically everyone in Charleston knows of Mrs. Emily Whaley. But even they may be in for a few surprises.

And Emily does love surprises.

Before meeting her for the first time I visited the garden. That was in October. A light rain was falling. I passed through the gate and the sounds of the city were suddenly muffled. The thick foliage of the entry glistened. I turned a corner and on all sides were what I noted at the time as "visual games." Flowers and shrubs and statuary and seashells and brick and wood and blue sky and water all played off of each other as they competed in turn for my attention. "Strong narrative," I wrote in my notebook. "A storyteller." I didn't know the half of it, for as you're about to see, Emily is a storyteller of the highest order. In the garden, a ramble along the paths brought

Mrs. Whaley and Her Charleston Garden

Gardening

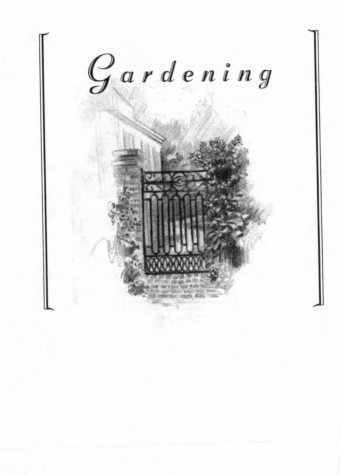

To Begin

I WAS BORN WITH A TRAIT I WOULDN'T GIVE UP FOR A MILLION DOLLARS. ENTHU-siasm. And I also have what the French call *joie de vivre*. As my middle daughter, Anne, says, "My God, Cheeka, you have an opinion on everything." I think they get fed up with my opinions, but where can you go in life without opinions?

Cheeka is what my family and friends call me. My father named me that. He held me up for my mother's inspection after I was born and said, "Nancy, looks like we have a che-week here." A cheweek is a waterbird a bit bigger than a sandpiper which we had around home. When my sister was born, he held her up and said, "This one's a peach." She was called Peach, which is far easier on you than being named for a waterbird. But I've been called Cheeka for more than eighty years, which is probably for the best. My real name is Emily, but my oldest daughter is "Miss Em" and I had an Aunt Em and now I have a granddaughter Emily. There are plenty of Emilys around.

I live in Charleston, South Carolina, on Church Street. My house dates from before the Revolutionary War and was owned by a signer of the Declaration of Independence. There's a plaque on the wall saying all that, so I won't add more. My husband, Ben Scott Whaley, and I moved here in 1938. The house is comfortable. It's one room wide but doesn't have the big piazzas the way the later single houses do.

Charleston. I assume everybody and their baby knows about Charleston. The Civil War started in the city's harbor, which is only a block over from our house. You won't hear about that from me, though. You won't hear about Church Street, either. If you know Charleston then you know Church Street. It's the oldest part of the city. Cabbage Row is just up the block. Cabbage Row was the Catfish Row of DuBose Heyward and George Gershwin's *Porgy and Bess*. The watercolorist Alice Smith had a studio a few doors away. Across the street is a Baptist church designed by Robert Mills, who was America's first architect. This is an ancient and colorful corner of the city, but I'm confessing to you now that most of the history you'll get from me is the family kind.

My friend Sally took me along with her once to give a garden lecture. I was just a warm body up there on the stage, but I thought I could handle it. When Sally finished speaking she asked for questions and the first one was "What year was the azalea introduced to Charleston?" I couldn't have answered that to save my blessed soul. I thought they'd be asking, "How do you grow an azalea?" Or, "How do you keep a cat out of your garden?"

So that's what I'll be attempting here. Not that I actually know how to keep a cat out of the garden, but gardening and gardens are central to this memoir. I have a garden that's pretty well known. It's small, only thirty feet wide and tucked

away in my backyard, but a great many visitors come, especially in the spring. Also, I'm going to say something about my parents and growing up in a little village to the north of the city. And I'll be giving out a few of those so numerous opinions, for what's the good of having an opinion if you don't share it with your friends and your wonderful daughters?

Junior

OR ME THE GARDENING YEAR BEGINS IN OCTOBER. THE HEAT OF THE SUMMER months is behind us and the days are beginning to sparkle. Long before the arrival of this special month I turn over in my mind what I am going to do in this area or that spot. Consider which new plants to try and those I will definitely get rid of. No artist ever says, "I'm going to paint a picture right now." Many thoughts go through his or her mind before the first stroke of paint is put to canvas, and so it is with the dedicated gardener and his or her plantings and compositions.

Inspiration is the bottom line. Without it the first move could not be made. We need to be led on bit by bit, by visits to gardens private and public, by garden tours, by immersing ourselves in illustrated garden books and catalogues. We see, absorb, winnow, and sift, and finally our imaginations take wing and out of all this come our gardening plans.

Number one on my late-October agenda is to clear out the two twenty-foot-long borders of all the summer flowers, most of which are still giving us a fine show. The minute I look the situation over, I begin to feel guilty and wasteful. They look so lovely, but I have allotted this morning to this project, and my gardener, Junior Robinson, is by my side. We both know that in a day or two frost will descend and have these lush beauties looking unhappy and faded. So I firm up my resolve, turn toward Junior, who's looking undecided, and tell him that we are going forward with this project now. I ask him if he wants a Classic Coke to strengthen him and he says, "Yes, I'm going to need it."

A warning: Life is full of decisions and you better not waver and quaver over each one or you will stress yourself. You will die young and miss your seventies and eighties, which are two decades that can be a delight.

Now, Junior, my ace in the hole, has the temperament and skills to be the perfect assistant for an eighty-five-year-old gardener. He is ever enthusiastic, optimistic, and patient. He says that what we do together is as much fun for him as it is for me. He moves around in a full flower border like a cat, never disturbing a plant. It is a feat, a gift from heaven, and almost

as rare an accomplishment as a lovely trained singing voice—
this surefooted agility is the first prerequisite you must look
for in anyone engaged to help you in your garden. "The best
laid schemes o' mice and men gang aft a'gley" if you have a
heavy-footed human being floundering around in your borders trying to be helpful. God forbid!

So, out go the geraniums and the petunias. Really it is quite
a relief to have it all empty and to have a totally unobstructed
view of the ornamental features that over the years have been
incorporated into the borders—urns, statues, birdbaths, and
raised areas. There is much detail that can be added to empha-
size balance and different levels, thus adding to the overall
interest of the garden.

We now check the condition of the background planting. A
dense, healthy group of evergreen plants is needed, but it
must not, under any circumstances, be allowed to outgrow
its allotted space, and it must look presentable after being
pruned. Every now and then you may have to replace a plant
that has lost its good looks through constant pruning with a
plant that is dense but grows more slowly.

In small gardens, if you are to keep your design in view and
also retain space for annuals and perennials, you have to move

in and do what is necessary to achieve this goal. This is part of the challenge of gardening. You not only want to grow healthy, beautiful plants and flowers, but you want to display them to their optimal advantage as well.

Every year, new plants are being offered by our nurseries and it is a morning's adventure to take off, by yourself, to ferret out the right plants for your composition. You can grow your plants from seed or from cuttings. You can get your "starts" from neighboring gardeners. To go all out, though, to simply walk into a nursery and say give me this and that, you need an ample supply of money. Gardening in this vernacular is not inexpensive. Though there are other ways to finance your gardening, one successful way is to choose carefully whom you marry. A good and generous man is needed, one who knows how to make money and enjoys sharing it, one who himself is not interested in the actual pursuit of gardening but likes to be proud of the premises.

Gardening is an art, just as painting is an art, and it is not likely that two people will collaborate happily in creating garden vignettes and vistas. If you are so lucky as to find such a man, you must fully realize and fully appreciate the fact that you have found a "pearl of great price." And if you think I have wandered away from the subject, you are mistaken. Before you begin to garden, figure out a way willy-nilly to finance an ongoing enterprise. Set aside your diamonds and racehorses. Budget where you can and put the money where your heart is. Gardening, to yield all of its pleasures, truly is an ongoing enterprise, one that will pay the best kind of dividends. It's a wonderful resource, one that develops your eye for beauty of all kinds — color, shape, design, and light. It provides an avenue to creativity. It entertains and it tempers stress. Plus it's always there for you. But don't forget, it's also there to be financed. I call that sort of commitment the importance of being earnest.

Having taken an objective view of gardening, let's proceed to the particular job at hand — the two twenty-foot-long borders that have just been cleared. Junior covers them with an inch of peat moss, a generous supply of Hoffman's super dehydrated cow manure, and a sprinkling of 5-10-5. He then turns this top dressing thoroughly in with a ten-inch fork. We water this down and let it rest for ten days.

Every year we try different selections of annuals and perennials. We have two goals in mind — first to achieve a harmonious color scheme for the flower borders and second to provide flowers for the house. This year, amongst other varieties, we planted calendulas. There is a new color in my dining room, soft apricot, and I thought the calendulas would be lovely in there.

When I am successful in both the garden and the house, I get the same satisfaction that a hunter feels when he sees a brace of succulent ducks, perfectly cooked, come to his dinner table, his guests oohing and aahing. He tells them of the beauty of first light on the marshes and how this pair of ducks wheeled into his blind at sixty miles an hour, how they chanced to cross right in front of him, and how he was able to bring the two of them down with one shot. "Yes!"

As my sparkling-eyed granddaughter Helen says when the basketball swishes through the net never touching the hoop —"Yes! Yes!"

Lovely fresh flowers for the house are for me the icing on the cake. When I walk into my parlor, the air perfumed with the fragrance from a vase full of our yellow roses, it's "Yes! Yes! Yes!"

Now, what can you do for your "pearl of great price" to make up to him for allowing you all of this freewheeling in your garden? For me it evolved that, amongst other things, he had the privilege of casting my vote, making it two votes from him on a regular basis, from dogcatcher to president. He also had his own refrigerator, which was his alone. In it there was always custard, made by the best custard maker in town— ME. I never felt it was an unfair exchange.

This was all back in the forties, fifties, sixties, and seventies, however. I have an idea it wouldn't fly so well today. No self-respecting woman, however uninformed she may be, would dream of giving up her personal vote. And, in addition, today there is such a flap about eggs and cholesterol that you would be suspected of trying surreptitiously to finish off a husband if you constantly provided custard.

So you will probably have to find a different sort of exchange, one that will be acceptable to both parties in the nineties. But don't get discouraged. There are many ways to share a garden with a mate, to get your interests fitting hand in glove. My parents did it one way. My husband and I did it another.

Mr. Briggs

URING JUNE AND JULY OF 1940, I WAS CONFINED TO BED FOR AN AIL-ment I needn't bore you with. Charleston was a steaming hot city and there was, of course, no air-conditioning. My husband, Ben Scott, wanted to divert me and one day asked if there were anything special he could do for my plea-sure. Well, I didn't have to give it a second thought. Would he have Mr. Loutrel Briggs make a design for our garden? Yes, gladly.

Our Church Street plot wasn't large—only 30 by 110 feet—but it had several natural advantages. It lay to the east of our house, which kept the hot afternoon sun from baking it. At the far end was the ancient high brick wall of a neighbor's carriage house. Plus there were sizable handsome trees in the lots to the left and right. A Charleston landscaper had done some work back there before we bought the house, but it didn't suit me. There was a large cedar taking up much of the area and the rest was bogged down in ligustrums. We asked Mr. Briggs to ignore all that and to draw up a perfect design for the area. We explained beforehand that the garden would be completed in sections—first because the children were young and they and their friends used three-fourths of the area for a playground and second because we had money enough only to get one section going. We would continue the project as the children outgrew the swings, sandbox, and basketball hoop, and as we had additional funds.

Mr. Briggs asked what type of garden we liked, formal or casual? How much area we wanted for bulbs, annuals, and perennials? How much for azaleas and camellias? Did we want a patio? Did we want plants to bloom over the whole year or did we prefer to concentrate the bloom during certain months of the year? We finally chose a romantic natural background with a formal foreground. Green predominates during the summer and early fall, while the bloom is concentrated from October through May.

That was it. In half an hour he formulated a plan and put it on paper. Gone was the forest of ragtag ligustrum and in its place a perfectly proportioned garden.

It began with a rectangle of lawn bordered by a walk and

flower beds on both sides. But the curved line was Mr. Briggs's true love and the rectangle spread into a circular shape with a round pool and statue at its center. This was to serve as the focal point for the formal half of the garden. A brick step raised the area around the pool and the walk remained slightly elevated until the natural half of the garden at the back was reached. At this point you stepped down into a large oval bounded at the far end by a rock-lined stream and encircled by azaleas.

I liked what I saw and told him so. In ten days or so he brought us a blueprint and also a colored-crayon sketch of what he thought the garden would look like in ten years' time. From then on we were on our own, which was probably for the best. You see, I was in awe of Mr. Briggs. He was by far the best-known landscape architect working around here. He had an international reputation. Born in Pennsylvania and educated at Cornell, he was the head of landscape architecture at the New York School of Fine Arts, had lectured all over the world, and had designed parks and public housing projects in New York City.

He'd first come to Charleston in 1929 and divided his time between here and New York. He did some wonderful projects

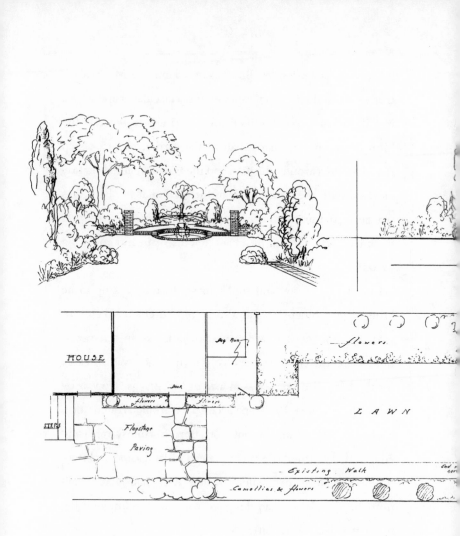

HOUSE

Dog Run

flowers

Door

flowers

flowers

STEPS

Flagstone
Paving

flowers

LAWN

Existing Walk

End of
new

Camellias & flowers

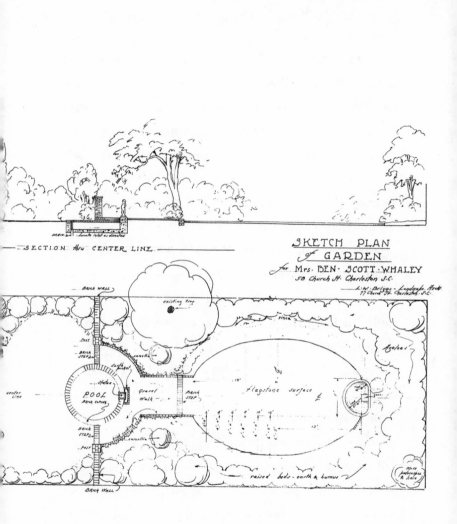

SECTION thru CENTER LINE

DRAIN and locate inlet as desired

SKETCH PLAN
of GARDEN
for Mrs· BEN· SCOTT· WHALEY
58 Church St· Charleston S.C.

L·W· Briggs - Landscape Arch.
77 Church St· Charleston, S.C.

BRICK WALL

existing tree

Vinca

Azaleas

BRICK
STEPS

camellia

earth bed

center
line

POOL
brick curing

Statue

Gravel
Walk

BRICK
STEP

flagstone surface

13'

13'

BRICK
STEPS

POST

camellia

brick curing

raised beds - earth & humus

More
landscaping
to here

BRICK WALL

[19]

around Charleston. He did Mepkin Plantation for Henry and Clare Booth Luce. That's Mepkin Abbey up by Moncks Corner. He also did gardens for Chicora Plantation and for Rice Hope, Bonny Hall, and Mulberry plantations, and landscape designs all along the coast—Georgetown and Myrtle Beach —and for a Marine Corps building on Parris Island. He did churchyards in Charleston and work on the campuses of both the College of Charleston and the Citadel. He did hundreds of private gardens in this area. He was a wonderful asset for Charleston, having ideas on everything from parking lots behind stores to a new street that would reduce the traffic along Charleston's main street. But I didn't really know much about all that. What I knew was that he had done gardens for my friends Sally and Sarah Lee that made me think I must have one, too.

Mr. Briggs didn't tell me what to plant. Not a strict listing anyway. In choosing our background plants we wanted a unified effect and therefore we used one variety of evergreen predominantly—pittosporum—and mixed in other varieties along the way. The dominance of pittosporum gives an echo all the way through the garden and induces a sense of serenity. This same plan was followed with the azaleas and then I added hydrangeas and yews and others. But I'll be returning to this later. In those first flower beds we concentrated on hyacinths, tulips, blue-and-white Dutch iris, violas, snapdragons, and stock. It is amazing how many you can squeeze in and what a succession of blooms you can achieve, but I'll return to this subject as well.

At the time, I thought Mr. Briggs had granted me this freedom with the planting because he didn't know what would grow in Charleston. I assumed he let everybody fill in his blueprint, but perhaps this was just for me. Maybe I was taking liberties. Brickwork was his trademark and one day Sally and I pulled up two chairs and watched the brick mason

working on the middle piers, which separate the two halves of the garden. We told him to make them lower than the plan showed. He didn't like the idea but did it anyway. We went along like that and when Mr. Briggs finally came around he took a long look and left without speaking. I guess he forgave me, though, because not so long after he said, "Emily, this garden of OURS is my favorite in Charleston." He returned a few years later to design a front section, and at the end of his career he listed my garden as one of the five best in the city.

Naturally, I'd seen plenty of gardens—been raised in gardens and come from a long, long line of gardeners. Years before, I'd even toured Europe with Aunt Em and Uncle Nick and seen gardens over there. Still, it wasn't until I saw Mr. Briggs's plan that I understood how you could conceal part of a garden. How you could have a place for herbs. A place for picking flowers. How you could plant surprises. And later I would follow up on this by adding vignettes myself and by adding the little lane at the back and the offset entry at the front.

Mr. Briggs said, "I don't like to do a garden for a person who is doing it because it's the thing to do or it's the period of the house." I agreed with him 100 percent and still do. I want a garden that's lived in. The thing I feel about a room is, if a room is not used it becomes insensitive. If a garden is not used it becomes insensitive. A garden has to be personal to work.

But having said that I can still spot a Briggs garden. I mean, no matter how intimate, no matter how personal the garden becomes, Briggs's handwriting, his outline, is still in evidence. It's not just in the details but in something as broad as the overall mood. You see, that's what he did for us. Separated the garden into two parts and then used the sun and shade to create differing moods in each. He had a gift. Size didn't matter. He could work on any scale. What he did was insist on making an imprint—bringing an order to the natural world.

Aunt Em said a garden should be enclosed. She said a garden pushed back the wilderness. A garden was an intimate ground safe from lions and elephants and whatever else was out there. It was a safe place outside and it needed to be enclosed to keep out the haints. Mr. Briggs agreed and that's what we have here. There are walls all around the garden. Still, I know from my own family's experience that gardens are impermanent. They can die with the owner. But at least one like this, with a solid floor plan laid down in brick, you always have it. A place that keeps out the lions and tigers. And my garden had an added benefit for my husband. As he was the first to point out, without it I'd have insisted on living in the country. I was from a long line of country gardeners and more than ready to follow in their happy footsteps. So Mr. Briggs's plan saved my husband from having to build a new house in the country and commute into Charleston to work.

The Belvidere Garden

HE FIRST OF MY MOTHER'S FAMILY, THE SINKLERS, SETTLED SIXTY MILES NORTH of Charleston on the Santee River. Heavy rains continually washed out their crops, however, so James and Peter Sinkler, who were brothers, moved just up-country. James and his wife built Belvidere in 1785—both house and garden—but the plantation was abandoned almost immediately and would not be reclaimed until my great-grandfather Charles Sinkler arrived in 1848. He'd been in the navy traveling the world over and back and had met and married Emily Wharton of Philadelphia. Lord knows this girl must have been an adventurer and Lord knows what her family thought. She'd been raised in the most cultivated city in America and here she was headed to the South, which had all its slavery problems. She was marrying a farmer and planning to live sixty miles from Charleston, South Carolina, in a place filled with mosquitoes. They must have thought she'd lost her mind. But she arrived and discovered a gay plantation life filled with horse races and music and happiness.

No one had been living at Belvidere when my great-grandmother Emily Wharton Sinkler first wrote to her father. Her letter said that the old garden was to be put back into condition. She said her husband, Charles, had given her a gardener and a carpenter for a month and that her hands were full and her life delightful. She said the weather was perfect.

Here is this young wife—the garden had been let go for decades—and here's this young wife in 1848 redoing that garden. Until it was flooded by Lake Marion about one hundred years later, the women in the Sinkler family would do their best to love and tend it. I don't know why there is such a yearning, but the women in my family have always been gardeners.

Though my great-grandmother got the garden into shape, her life would end sadly. She had five children. The only way her family in Philadelphia would sanction the marriage was if she promised to return north to give birth to her children. She did this and all had reached their teens safely. One Sunday, however, the family was driving back to Belvidere from the

Rocks Church. They passed by Eutaw Springs. Something frightened the horses and they got away from Mr. Sinkler. The buggy wheel hit a pine root and Emily was thrown into a tree and killed immediately. How dreadful it must have been.

Charles died not many years after Emily and Belvidere passed to their youngest son, Charles St. George Sinkler, and his wife, Anne Porcher Sinkler, who were my grandparents —and Anne loved and nurtured the garden. Now this was after the Civil War, but most of the freed slaves still lived on the plantation. One of these, Daddy Lewis, became my grandmother Anne's full-time gardener. Theirs was a happy meeting of two congenial souls. His house was ten feet from the back garden gates and just across the lane from the big stable yard. These circumstances—a knowledgeable owner-director, a resident gardener, and a handy supply of manure—produced a flourishing garden. Anne not only had a vision of what the garden should be, but she also had the skill and patience to bring it to birth and follow through with the maintenance. In addition to all this, as Daddy Lewis's house began to fill with babies and little children, the garden became a happy sanctuary for him. He could be found there from dawn to dusk, hoeing, digging, planting, fertilizing, admiring, enjoying, and resting. He gave a sensitive and loved feel to the garden that comes only through constant loving attention to detail. My grandmother Anne shared this with him.

The Belvidere garden was big enough to include both flowers and vegetables and was completely enclosed by a brick and wrought-iron fence that kept out the flock of sheep that grazed the big lawn. The garden had a very formal European layout. You entered through a wide front gate opening onto a long, ten-foot-wide path that led to the very back of the garden. There was an equally wide path that crossed the main path at its midpoint, and off these two main paths the quartered garden was further divided into small areas. The flowers were on the left as you entered.

There were rose arbors covered with Cherokee and Lady Banksia roses. Then, in the most open and uninterrupted sunlight, were the old-fashioned bush roses like Duchess of Brabant. And in the center of these roses was a sundial. And rimming all these roses were blue flags.

Along the sides of the main paths were all the old favorites, banana shrub, gardenias, forsythia, weigela, bridal wreath, and sweet olive. Always my most favorite was a white double-flowering peach. It stunned me as a child, hypnotized me with its beauty. The perimeter path around this entire side of the garden was devoted to more blue flags.

I guess I should explain that flags are our native irises. My daughter Marty painted a watercolor of those Belvidere flags. Now when I think of Belvidere I think of her picture. I've tried planting flags myself, but I have too much shade. Sun is all they need, really. Flags are like the Cherokee roses. You see them growing in ditches and all about, but they were domesticated in the beginning. Blue flags. Perfectly charming, that entire garden. Sustenance for both body and soul and a lesson for the young. My mother, Nan, and her two sisters were willing pupils.

Nan grew up in the Belvidere garden (and in the nearby stable yard). Her sister, my Aunt Em, tended the mushrooms. Their mother, Anne, tended the asparagus. And Daddy Lewis watched over all of it. You know, when you garden with a person on a regular basis you become very close. You're doing something, the two of you are a team. Grandmother had Daddy Lewis. They were devoted friends and when she died at the early age of fifty-four he grieved perfectly terribly. He had no direction and then one day he said to my mother, who was married by then, "Miss Anne (most people knew her as

Miss Anne, not as Nan), Old Missy come back to me yesterday while I was sitting in the garden late in the evening. She
appeared to me and says you have got to stop grieving after
me. You are keeping me from being at ease. I'm in a good
place where you don't need to worry."

Nan's father had been invalided by fever long before this, so
when her mother died she took over the garden and the running of all the rest of Belvidere. She'd come over the twenty
miles from Pinopolis once a week and sometimes I'd go along.
She had nurses for her father and had a doctor from Eutaw-
ville to tend to the health of all the blacks on the plantation.
Growing up she had been a favorite on the plantation "street,"
attending the weddings and funerals of the black residents and
every Sunday going with them to their little church on the hill.

Nan had hired a young man who lived on an adjacent plan-
tation to help with the crops at Belvidere. Relatives from
Pennsylvania shared the expenses and came for holidays.
There were cattle and that flock of sheep to keep fenced out.
I remember roses being propagated under glass jars there.
Those old-fashioned roses were tough. Louis Philip and Chero-
kee roses. On the dining table there were very simple crystal
pitchers filled with Duchess of Brabant roses. Pale pink. A

blushing pink. Perfectly lovely with a bloom no more than an inch and a half across and the most delicious fragrance.

But what I want you to understand is that my mother and both my aunts were lifelong gardeners, and the women of the next generation were gardeners, too.

A Gardening Glossary

If you are a novice,
as I take you to be,
you'll neither know nor understand
unless you can easily see.
So put your hand in ours
and we'll take it page by page,
and before you'll fully know it,
you'll be a gardening sage.

E'RE ALMOST READY FOR A TOUR OF MY GARDEN, AN APRIL TOUR to be exact. But first we have some loose ends to tie and some basic definitions and vocabulary to go over. I want us to be speaking the same language and I'm hoping it's gardener's English.

The United States is divided into gardening ZONES. Mostly this has to with temperature. Charleston, South Carolina, is zone 9, and I try to stick with plants that are recommended for that climate. That means no peonies or rhododendrons—

a sad deprivation. But we can grow the camellias, oleanders, and parkinsonias that others are denied. Your supplier can help you here. Also, there are garden clubs everywhere waiting to tell you what and how to plant. Ireland, Persia, Italy, Maine, and Texas. Yes! They are all fine places to garden, but most of my opinions are based on the spot I know best, the coastal region of South Carolina.

A BOUNDARY or SCREEN PLANTING encloses your haven. It marks the line across which no alien creature—strange dogs and cats or prying humans—may intrude. It's a screen behind which you enjoy seclusion's pleasures—sunbathing, loafing, thinking, flirting, or stargazing. Plus it's the backdrop for all your design elements. Make it of a vigorously growing collection of several plants and trees of various heights and shapes. Let one evergreen predominate—something to carry the burden and provide a sense of unity.

The lower ten feet should be the densest. I suggest mixing the shapes. Round and dark like azaleas, pittosporum, myrtle, or oleanders for Charleston. And vertical such as yew, cyclera, camellias, bay, and my favorite, Italian cypresses. The upper ten to twenty feet can include both deciduous and evergreen trees that are small. Down here in South Carolina, the first type includes dogwood, crepe myrtle, parkinsonia, vitex, and pink bud. All these bloom in the spring and change leaf color in the fall. Important since you want color as high up as possible. The small evergreen trees I can grow include ligustrum, photinias, cherry laurel, and bays for blooming in the spring, and loquat and sweet olive for the fall and winter blooms.

Often in town gardens you'll have a garden wall or house wall to aid in the quest for seclusion, but remember, these need help as well. Border planting is still needed to break up these large expanses of masonry or wood. And of course you may wish to screen off separate sections of the garden itself—to divide the cookout area from the rose garden or herb garden. Plants can easily edge and define these islands of interest.

Neither a borrower nor a lender be, for loan oft loses both itself and friend. Except when you're talking about BOR-ROWED LANDSCAPING. If you're thinking of purchasing a piece of town or city property or have made up your mind to fix up the one you've got, study the yard with notebook in hand. Walk slowly around the perimeter examining that magic space above ten feet. What do you see up there that could add charm to the scene? Church steeple? Tiled roof? Chimney? House gable or handsome tree? These not-for-sale beauties are called borrowed landscaping. When you plan your garden, you want the views of the borrowed landscape to be unobstructed. In fact, your planting should draw attention to them. And while you have out the notebook, list the minuses —things to *un*borrow. The unadorned edges of houses, intrusive windows, electricity and telephone poles and their wires. You can screen these from view. Dogwood, loquat, and ligustrum block well. A palmetto tree or cypress or cedar can lend its column shape to screen that pole.

And what about those unsightly sights in your own yard? Note the concrete drive or garage entrance. These may be necessary, but do you care to see them from the house or garden? Study the view from the important windows of the house and decide if medium-sized plants like myrtles, azaleas, boxwood, or fatsia can help to screen these spots.

The FLOOR PLAN. Every house with a floor has one. Gardens have them too. I had a professional landscaper start me off. It helps to get the proper proportions right from the beginning, but if you've got a yen to do your own thing, don't hesitate. Take hold of the pen and pad. Grab up the yardstick and string and let your own eye do the planning.

The FOCAL POINT, as the name implies, is the center of

interest. The most important feature of your garden, it must be clearly established in order to bring a feeling of order and unity. A statue of the right dimensions or a birdbath, a gazebo or bench or an unusually sculpted eye-catching plant—there are many options but the choice must immediately draw your eye toward it. Remember, without a focal point a garden can quickly dissolve into a hodgepodge of plants that have no reason for being there. Plan ahead. Not just with the focal point but with all the elements. Don't just shop on impulse and then come home and stick plants, birdbaths, or statuary in any available space. Plan ahead before you spend that money. Self-discipline is needed!

For the word VIGNETTE I'll let my dictionary do the work: "A vignette is an ornamental or decorative design, usually of a relatively small size, unenclosed in a border and having its

edges shading off into the surrounding area or background."
Akin to focal points (for which they can sometimes double),
vignettes also need a central element. A statue, rock, or any
small plant—fern, violets, or violas, or a mixture of whatever
appeals—is at the center of this little picture. Vignettes form
a secondary interest. A conversation piece. They break up the
monotony of a border planting and help you organize on either
side. If you make vignettes your specialty, a casual visitor will
have the impression of strolling in an outdoor art gallery.

VISTA is another one I'll take from the dictionary: "A view
or prospect seen through an avenue of trees or other long and
narrow opening—a mental view or vision of far-reaching
nature." Well, the very word puts my imagination into high
gear. A vista is a view that is framed, and it can be as close as
the end of your garden or as far away as the stars. Of course,
the shorter of these two views has the advantage of being
composed, controlled, and cared for by the garden owner. A
bit farther away and you may be seeing a church steeple,
ocean, river, or mountain. But here you are at the mercy of
your neighbors' trees, while the heavens are for everybody
and everyday. Sunrises and sunsets. Blue skies and night skies.
Silver-lined clouds and dramatic dark storms. And you may

add in pelicans, herons, robins, or cedar waxwings making a passage across your vista. Near or far we earthbound souls must understand. A vista adds dimension to your life. It's an avenue to beauty and a reminder that it's a joy to be alive.

Well-placed SEATING is an indispensable part of the garden. Place it singly for a secluded retreat or grouped together for friends and family. And make it comfortable—a chair or bench that invites you to sit longer and meditate or chat. Of course, each type of garden, or each space within a garden, requires a suitable style of furniture. I use iron park benches with wooden slats, which are familiar to Charlestonians. Junior says he's getting too old to move them, which would be a tragedy, because I still enjoy shifting them about, experimenting as you would with household furniture. In and out of the shade as the seasons change or off to where the blooms and views are presently the best. Remember, the seating can (and should) be moved.

People generally think of having PICNICS in far-off lovely spots—by tumbling waterfalls or still ponds, on mountainsides with distant views. These are certainly treats to remember, but picnics in the garden should not be overlooked. You should be aware, though, that there are those who hope very much that you will not embarrass them by inviting them to such an unpleasant occasion. Either by imagination or unfortunate experience, they are led to believe that there are more ants and buzzing and biting insects in a garden than there are flowers. Choose your guests carefully, and for safety have a can of Off handy. If you provide yourself with a few simple picnic conveniences, you will find that you'll not only give pleasure to your friends but will do so often. Here is a list of basics that make it all doable.

1 basket with paper plates, napkins, plastic glasses and forks, and a corkscrew

1 basket with sandwiches

1 basket with melon balls, strawberries, grapes, and chunks of pineapple

3 or 4 very small baskets with a variety of cookies or candy, placed near your guests

Also have an ice chest to keep wine and juices cold. And last but not least, have a pretty can with a cover for trash—empty plates, glasses, bottle tops, and cans. Cleanup will be easy. Most people enjoy seeing what grows in other people's gardens. Most people love to eat what someone else has fixed. Your guests will thank you for a good, convivial time.

COLOR. A matter of pleasure and some confusion for most gardeners. Even though Monet used red successfully in his color schemes, and even though men count on red roses to facilitate their communication with women—from proposals to apologies—I still think red is a difficult color to include in central flower border schemes. It seems to catch the eye and hold it, thus diminishing the value of the flowers adjacent. Remember: A good blue can fix anything.

Some years ago, I decided my handling of color simply wasn't working—all too spotty and uncoordinated. I was mixing two color fields, each lovely by itself but disastrous when combined. So I learned to choose one color field per season and stick with it: either the pure pinks, blues, lavenders, and purples or the peach and apricot-to-salmon colors. I start with the azaleas, which bloom first. The tulips are bought to blend in, and then the geraniums for the tulips, and the chrysanthemums are keyed to these. Of course, within each color field you have different tones and hues, from dark to light, which give a rich harmony to all. Well, you might not agree with a word of this, but it's certainly simpler than random guessing. The fun, after all, is in getting color choices to work. When you find a successful combination, record it for the future. When you're visiting other gardens, jot down the color combinations that appeal to you. Don't rely on memory. Keep a notebook!

There are all kinds of books on managing time and saving time, but we should be learning how to enjoy time or, more exactly, how to time our enjoyment. Remember your TIMES OF PEAK BLOOM. Have the garden at its best during the time you use it most. In the coastal southeast, the summer months are hot and humid and our gardens are home-sweet-home to numerous pesky mosquitoes. During this time, I simply try to keep the vines and volunteers under control. But that's for me in the city. If you're in the cooler countryside or where the sea breezes blow, you may want to plant daylilies, phlox, cleome, and shasta daisies.

For Charleston gardens the fall is better — October, November, and the first part of December. Blue plumbago and gerbera daisies are a must, and roses give a good account. The lavender lantana and the lavender false dragonhead blend well with the plumbago and gerberas. Pentas, which come in pink, lavender, blue, and white, are excellent for the fall.

Camellias start in December and the sweet olive, too. Those hardest winter months aren't suitable for sitting out, but we enjoy a stroll. And spring is not so far behind. That's the peak blooming time for my garden. First dogwoods, azaleas, tulips, roses, pansies, and so much more. Then, in May, the blue hydrangeas, the yellow parkinsonia, the oleanders, and the blue vitex and daylilies. Which brings the garden color back to mid-June.

WATER can be still or moving or a bit of both. A still surface provides a soothing ambience. It brings a quiet to all that surrounds. It mirrors shapes and colors and even movement. And still water is a magnet. It draws in not only thoughts of quiet and calm but a veritable host of animals as well. Birds come to drink, bathe, and teach their young about the world.

Frogs sing as though onstage. Dragonflies skim the surface, dipping low for a taste of cool water. A cat slinks by with predatory designs on a curious lizard. And squirrels and darting hummingbirds that seem so intensely busy still have time to pass that way. And of course there's my Jack Russell terrier, Rosie, who just yesterday went sliding into the reflecting pool in pursuit of a mocking, strutting bird (too late, of course).

Moving water tumbles, twirls, and twinkles over rocks and swirls around mossy curves. (Junior sees to this with his pumps and hoses hidden inside the pools and tiny waterfalls.) Moving water sparkles and offers lovely sounds. Birds wade in the water and Rosie slips and slides in it as well. And all these tiny adventures remind us that we're not alone. Not in this garden or on this planet either.

Everything we use in a garden either adds or takes away from its beauty. There are no neutrals, and POTS and CONTAINERS are no exception. As a rule, I prefer the simple clay ones of varying depths, shapes, and sizes, rather than the inexpensive but overdecorated concrete ones or the ponderous wooden ones. Not that I'm opposed to style and quality, but the really beautiful containers are expensive. Mention them in your letter to Santa Claus or speak yearningly of them when birthdays or anniversaries approach. Make sure everyone knows that these are the best of all substitutes for those long-stemmed red roses, half of which never open anyway! Or treat yourself if you must. A planting in a handsome urn or other container is like an eye-catching Easter hat, and the ultimate treat for the eye of the beholder.

If you enjoy COLLECTING as I do, then the garden is just the place to indulge this very basic instinct. Ivies are an easy start. There are at least a half-dozen varieties of widely varying colors, sizes, and leaf shapes. And all can succeed in those difficult places (high or low) where other plants do poorly. Try the variegated ivies in conjunction with the solid-colored varieties. Climb fences with them or use them as ground cover alongside a path or the driveway. Don't be afraid of ivies. Unlike kudzu they can be stopped. Ferns are another simple collectible. You can dig them from the woods or a neighbor's yard and mix and match to please. But to me the real challenge for collecting are the camellias and roses. But more of that elsewhere.

PRUNING must be constant and judicious. I never walk into my garden without my clippers in hand, ready to snip any and every ambitious tendril that is trying to sneak out of its allotted space. To do this effectively, you need to have a one-on-one relationship with the plants in your garden. This practice avoids a great deal of troublesome heavy pruning later on, when plants are allowed to have their way, run rampant over everything, and get completely out of shape and control. If you can't do the major pruning yourself, be certain that you stand within five feet of the person doing it and that you have your mind and eye focused on the job. Another human being does not have the same picture in his or her mind of what the garden needs and can unintentionally wreck your personal picture and plans.

Keep an eagle eye out and don't hesitate to REPLANT. I have noticed that even though a plant may have looked healthy when bought and be suited for your locality, sometimes it just will not thrive. Give it two years and no longer. If by then it still looks seedy, going backward instead of forward, and you're convinced it won't ever be happy, don't try to doctor it back to health. Don't even wait the two years. It won't ever be a thing of beauty, so get rid of it. That's called unsentimental gardening.

And now if you understand all of the above and have no questions (How could you have questions? I've made you a gardening sage, haven't I?), it's time for an April tour.

My Garden

HERE'S A TOUR OF MY OWN GARDEN. IT'S AN IMAGINED TOUR COMPOSED of words. So you must use your imagination and must begin by imagining that it is that most beautiful of months in Charleston—April. The temperature is seventy degrees and the sky bright blue with just a scattering of wispy clouds. A light breeze is blowing. You are well rested and well fed and happy to be alive. And I am happy to have you as a guest. Come along.

I'll start by pointing out the doorway of my neighbor directly across the street. This will be your focal point coming out of my gate. That's right. Remember that a garden has to work in two directions. Your eye is directed one way as you walk in and the opposite way as you come out. That door is the last thing you see on leaving and it is absolutely beautiful—planted all around with Ballerina roses and Confederate jasmine. That's the ultimate in borrowed landscap-

ing, because that door is the most photographed door not just in Charleston but in all of America. I'll bet it with money. Now on with the tour.

The entry to my garden is formed by the front wall and doorway of my house and the back wall of my next-door neighbor's house. It's a narrow space, no wider than six feet in places and paved over with brick, except in a couple of places where the bricks have been removed to accommodate big plants. We've bordered this planted area with more brick laid in a scalloped pattern. It's an illusion, you see. The solid brick pavement now appears to be a slightly winding path leading up to the garden gate.

Another trick we've used in this entry area is potted plants, both standing and hanging. We've done this partly because the area is paved and partly because of the freedom it gives. I've got sweet olive by the front door. It's doing double duty, serving both the front door and the garden entry beside it, and it offers a delicious smell. I'm about to plant Confederate jasmine here as well.

You're in luck, all right. The last week in April and the first in May are the most beautiful time for Charleston. The jasmine is blooming and so are the roses and the oleander. The parkinsonia too. There's no better time for the tourist to see the parkinsonia. And it's not the best time just for private gardens. During those two weeks the whole city is a garden. My mother used to say that Charleston in May is like an exquisite young bride.

But to return to the more mundane. I use, as I said, mostly clay pots. You don't have much trouble with them freezing in Charleston. It's a rare occasion when it goes down to ten degrees. I've got one big wooden container that does have the advantage of size, but it's rotting away at the bottom and difficult to move. And you do want to be able to move these pots to adjust the color. As blooms come and go, just a few inches can make a difference.

There are plenty of gardens in Charleston no bigger than my narrow entry and many of these are paved solid as well. You can garden just with pots. Remember: Geraniums and impatiens pay you back in spades. They thrive in pots and bloom for the longest time. And in pots or out of them they give color you can count on. If you're opening your garden to tours this is particularly important. But be careful. Be tasteful. Sometimes you can have too much of a good thing.

Next we come to the gate. It's wrought iron. You can see

through it and to the garden that beckons beyond. Wrought iron says Charleston. New Orleans has the wrought-iron balconies. Ours don't compare in comfort or in safety. I always have the feeling that Charleston balconies are stuck on, more decorative than useful. But we have the more beautiful gates. There are craftsmen like Philip Simons still doing this kind of work. Yes, wrought iron says Charleston. And best of all, the old gate was here when we bought the house.

When I came out this morning there was a "start"—a cutting—wrapped and waiting here at the gate. In Pinopolis and on the plantations, everybody's garden was very much like everybody else's because everybody gave everybody a start of everything. But I was happy to get this one. Verbena. My neighbor was saying, "Here, I brought you a present and there are lots of varieties of verbena, so I know I won't be duplicating."

Stepping through the gate we reach a short dogleg path. It's paved with flagstones instead of brick and here the plants increase in size, creating a green wall that blocks the view of the main garden ahead. Hydrangea and azaleas and variegated pittosporum. For the hydrangeas—with their lace-cap bloom—I prefer the pinks, lavenders, and blues, but not the really deep blues. Lime in the soil gives you pink. Rusty nails planted about the roots make a blue flower. The azaleas mostly have large blooms—some bright pink, some lavender—but to the left is a miniature Japanese variety that blooms on Mother's Day. Of course, there's more. Ferns and clethra. Clematis. You're seeing dozens and dozens of leaf shapes in just these few first steps, but we are still controlling the space and creating a sense of continuity by repeating the larger evergreens. There's a yew and another yew. Then a loquat and another and another and we've done the same with the hydrangea and azaleas and camellias, which go all the way through to the end of the garden. This gives you a sense of serenity. A sense of security. This is pretty basic. You want to give variety but also to avoid that uncomfortable mixing up. You want it interesting but at the same time you should retain a feeling of familiarity. Echoes. I believe that word suits.

These boxwoods were a gift from Junior. Hurricane Hugo flooded this entire end of Charleston in 1989. Saltwater three feet deep and it settled in odd pockets. It killed six of the box on the right side of the entry. They were special and hard to find, but Junior told me not to worry and the next day here were six more. He'd dug them up from his own yard and he said, "My wife's going to kill me, but you need them more than me"—which I think was very loyal of him and very brave.

The loquats almost dominate here. They have a tropical feel with that broad leaf and round, burnished orange–colored fruit that's very good tasting. An evergreen. They bloom in October and November. They suit Charleston. I used to keep them espaliered, clipped up flat against the stuccoed back wall of my neighbor's house, but a bad freeze killed off the truly big ones. In fact, the large containers I'm using in this area cover up their stumps. This is as far north as they'll do.

Then along comes a storm with widespread destruction,
From chaos comes the chance for bold reconstruction,
To express a new person despite what befalls,
With no fire of London, there'd be no St. Paul's.

Francis Underhill, a friend and newspaper columnist, said that about storms. It's absolutely true. Ice or wind. Heat or flood. Sometimes nature does our sculpting for us. My oldest daughter, Miss Em, had a beautiful yard and Hurricane Hugo destroyed everything. Blew down all these tremendous long-leaf pines, but I've helped her to rebuild. Junior and I go out to help. Now she and her husband, Grant Whipple, have put all that new sunlight to work growing roses—storybook roses —the kind you think grow only in magazine pictures. And we've put in a forest of Chinese tallow. We planted little twigs and in seven years some are already twenty feet tall.

Now back to our April tour. Fatsia is another favorite here in the dogleg. I like the shiny leaf. That's a screening leaf. You can garden with leaves, which is what I'm doing for most of this stretch. There's Irish yew, particularly easy to keep clipped, and four other yews as well. They're all evergreens. Short leaves, long leaves, waxy and flat, slow growing and fast and it's all still yews.

And facing the visitor is a small statue. A maid with pitcher. It came from a garden supply store and had a bright white finish. Just concrete but I let it mellow. It gained a patina from the weather and lost that crass whiteness. Nowadays, original pieces of statuary are just too expensive, but I've found a wonderful source for the inexpensive concrete variety. It's at the end of a winding mountain road. Migrant workers make the statues in the off-season and all this Latin music is playing. That place is a concrete world. You can find *The Thinker* and leprechauns sitting on toadstools. I mean some of it is perfectly awful, but you can get excellent buys there as well.

The last original piece of sculpture I bought was years ago. One of Hirsch's (a local sculptor who's very well known). It was a baby looking into a pool of water, but it was broken in a storm. Now I've got all these others. Inexpensive and attractive but my children think it's too much. Well, it's all a matter of taste and even the beautiful might not work. If everyone's using the same piece, it's hackneyed. There's such a thing as too many dancing girls. But I'm happy. I've got a couple of lead pieces left. The two dogs and the duck in the reflecting pool. The little fox is terra-cotta. The rest are concrete.

Of course, a focal point can be anything that draws your attention. Plants like Spanish bayonet. That's a striking example. It grows on the sea islands around here. A sculpted plant with spikes that will half kill you if they stick, and out of the center this big white bloom in the spring. A sago palm could work as well. There's a beautiful one by the Presbyterian church and another on South Battery. A plant can draw your attention. Topiary could even serve as a focal point. We think most often of statuary, but it could be seashells too. I could pile up seashells. Junior brought me some conches recently. A focal point can be anything. Just remember that it must work for the return trip as well.

On our right I painted an arch on the stucco of my neighbor's wall and then laid a wicker lattice over that. You can't always count on plants alone to decorate your boundaries. Now we take a sharp left here and then we can see the main garden. That's the purpose of the dogleg. To create this surprise and put visitors exactly where we want them. Mr. Briggs said to use every square foot of the garden and that's what I'm doing.

At this point we've got the old back-porch steps behind us. They're made of the original brick and I left them when the porch got glassed in. The steps themselves are the setting for a vignette—a small composition to one side. A small statue of a laughing child is on the top step and below it is an odd assortment of seashells and ferns. The tiny shells were brought by my children from an Isle of Palms vacation. The bigger shells were from a house party on Bulls Island. Those are little gray rocks from the coast of Maine where my daughter Miss Em has a house. The steps are like a waterfall—of vegetation and remembrances. The ferns are planted at the top and then seed themselves down the rest of the way. Not just the bigger ferns but also the tiny brackens. Of course, you must prune these as well. Pull them free of their purchase

or you lose the composition very quickly. The steps are not just a vignette seen off to one side. When you're leaving the garden they're the main focal point in the retreat.

Now we have you at the optimum point. If you've got the steps behind you, you're looking down the main axis of the garden and seeing it at its most beautiful. If you glance to your right there's another vignette. A heron fishing in a shallow pool and Japanese lanterns surrounding that centerpiece. The camellias bordering the pool drop their petals on the water. Papyrus at the edge. That's what Moses was hidden in, that and bulrushes on the river Nile. Holly ferns circle behind. They need shade so they do great in Charleston. Sometimes they push too far and it's easy for spots like this to get overrun and lost. Also in here is a bit of wilderness. Hercules-club and a circle of ginger brought in from the swamps of Berkeley County. Also some mother-of-thousands, which was a gift from a Charlestonian. It's a ruthless spreader, as the name suggests. The ginger, with that heart-shaped leaf, is a ground cover taken straight from our swamps. The ginger is a bit rare and needs my help to show. The Hercules-club gets its name from all those spines. They're dramatically revealed in the bareness of winter and have rich orange leaves in the fall. You want to bring these wild things in when they're dormant, which means in December and January. I don't prune when transplanting from the woods because you lose the plant's natural shape. Odd to say, my mother felt the opposite and transplanted from the wild with bare root and cut-back branches.

To the left, where Ben Scott once had his dog pens, is the lattice-covered storage area designed by Mr. Briggs. This is a place to hide away the tools and fertilizer and it's also an entry to the kitchen. You need this sort of easy access to your tools, but unfortunately several other people have easy access to them as well and at this moment I don't own a shovel. No shovel on this whole damn place.

Also to the left but a step farther on is a seating area. Garden chairs and a bench of iron and wood and a small marble-topped table. A perfect spot to entertain friends. The kitchen door is just a few steps away and there's a great view of the garden's central axis. I've got clay pots decorating this area as well. Tremendous ones because they're holding roses. A rose takes a big pot, but I'd have to dig through the flagstones to plant them, and a pot gives the added advantage of raising the color level. You can simply set the pot on a stump or holder and have instant color at eye level. And for scent and foliage there's sweet olive and eucalyptus. That's the same sweet olive that's by the front door. It's also called tea olive. It blooms off and on all winter. A tiny white flower whose petal has the same thick velvety texture of the jasmine and banana shrub blooms. Or the magnolia. And the aroma is unbelievable.

We turn away from the seating area and once more are standing at the central axis of the garden, about to enter what Mr. Briggs first designed. At our feet, a twenty-five-by-twelve-foot rectangle of grass bordered by a narrow brick path, and between the path and my neighbor's wall, flower beds of annuals and perennials and larger boundary plantings. The grass is a must-have. We want our flower beds overflowing with the colors of the rainbow, but a garden is also a place of repose and order. Grass is the answer. Think about it. Grass is all one color and every leaf is the same shape and cut to the same height. It's smooth and velvety and gives the area a distinctly defined edge. In short, grass is a resting place. I don't mean a place for Rosie to roll on her back, though she might. Grass is a reprieve for the eye and mind.

Now it would be perfect if nothing heavier than a mockingbird's foot should ever fall upon your grass, but that won't happen. You nurture this green space like it was a babe in swaddling bands, feed it on a regular schedule, and when water doesn't come from the heavens, you supply it from below. You do all that, but still visitors are tempted to take a shortcut, and here—where the traffic is heaviest—it's hardest to keep them off. That's why Junior and I are trying a little experiment. He's brought in these beautiful white conches and we've arranged them in patterns and buried them in the lawn with the spines facing up. No. They won't maim anyone permanently, but very clearly they are saying DON'T STEP ON US.

To continue. Fortunately for me the yard lies along an east–west axis, so we have sun on one side and shade on the other. Of course, that means the garden can't be perfectly symmetrical. The left and right can't match. If I want the tulips on each side to bloom the same week, I have to plant the sunny left side two weeks after the right side. But that's good. Having it all the same would be dull and this way we get to play around. Roses in the sun and camellias in the shade, but still the illusion of symmetry.

At the far end of the grass rectangle, the brick curves in to embrace the statue and reflecting pool—our focal point here. The statue is of a child struggling with a duck and two more ducklings look on from the pool. Mr. Briggs designed a deep pool, but I had little children then and had him stop it at just one inch, which works fine. The light is reflected just the same and the birds love it. Yesterday afternoon I was sitting out here with Rosie beside me. Now, Rosie is scared to death of water. If somebody even touches a hose she's long gone. Well, there's a bird walking through the pool in the most confident way. The bird must have lost its mind. It walks to the edge and Rosie is after it before its foot touches dry land. The bird barely escapes. Rosie is five. At least I'm going to say she's five. She might want to lie about her age. And since I don't want her to get old, I'll fib about it for her.

To get back to the tour. Circles were important to Mr. Briggs. The shape is repeated in this reflecting pool, of course, and then in the portion of garden ahead of us, and here at the start you see the circle motif in the rounded boxwoods. On the right I've got digitalis in the shade and, higher up, cosmos and roses in the sun. That highest rose is a Mermaid. That's a single rose with a pale yellow bloom. Vigorous. Yes, indeed. I was once told that no garden is a real garden without a Mermaid rose. And I figured if one was good, I'd get five. I was inundated with Mermaid roses. Now I'm back to one. The planting on that side is dense to a height of ten feet. If I went higher I'd block the sun from my sunny side. You want privacy but have to watch out for the shade. And planted along the farthermost boundary line are Italian cypresses, four on each side. They're tall and spindly spires. Striking in shape, and they create a visual block. The garden is also graced by a collection of twenty-five beautiful old camellias, an evergreen shrub that has been a boon to South Carolina gardeners for centuries. The varieties I have in my garden are pink perfection, white queen, and spring sonnet,

among others. These camellias, along with several other ever-green plants and the eight Italian cypresses, form the screen that provides the garden with a sense of privacy and gives a uni-fied effect to the overall scene. If you concentrate, you can eas-ily look past the cypresses, but the eye doesn't work that way. We see the cypresses and ignore most of what's beyond. Mine are getting a bit long of tooth. They grow surprisingly fast and people are saying replace them—but they're awfully expensive.

Another aid to privacy is the scalloped wooden fence that was here when I arrived. I kept it, which may have been a mis-take, because the wood was not treated and it has been slowly rotting. Remember this sad fact. Most workmen simply don't care. When your garden is at its best is when they decide to show up and it's all of utter unimportance to them. Still, I should take that fence down and rebuild out of treated lum-ber. Also, the fence is painted white, which is often recom-mended as a way to show off your blooms. I don't agree and try to keep the greenery covering up all but the top—the scallops, posts, and finials.

We'll take the brick path toward the rear. Remember this: Paths are the routes of the explorer. They give us that one-on-one relationship with the plants. I built my paths out of brick and flagstone because that suits Charleston and complements the garden. The important thing is to keep paths narrow in a town garden. Mine are no more than twenty inches wide. It's a privilege to walk single file. Suppose you're walking two abreast. You're seeing only half the view. That may sound selfish, but if you're an avid gardener you want your full attention on the garden. Yes. I realize we're doing this tour together, but you're imaginary and therefore take up very little room and block out absolutely nothing.

This sunny bed to the left is the brightest and the best for the cut flowers and for simply showing off. Right at the start is a snowdrop lily. I've got a couple of truly ancient camellias, but I believe this snowdrop has been here since Charleston has been here. I bet it came in 1680 from the other side of the ocean—from the snowfields of the Himalayas. It was the same size when I came here almost sixty years ago. Heavy green stem about six inches tall and the snowdrops on the end—tiny white bells with tinier green dots on them.

I had pansies—mixed blue and yellow—in strawberry jars here all winter and tulips of a red I didn't order this spring. They won't take the heat and both have just been removed. I should take this opportunity to tell you about tulips. The heat here in Charleston is a problem. Some people keep the bulbs from year to year. They dig them up and hang them in nylon stockings. I never do. Most daffodils come back. At the end of three years you can divide them. The little jonquils come back. But I never take the least effort to make the tulips come back because they'll be half the size. You can try putting the bulbs in the refrigerator, but it doesn't work for me. I just consider tulips a luxury. A big chocolate cake doesn't last either. It's a luxury and you eat it once. Some things are a luxury. You wear a wedding dress once. You plant tulip bulbs once.

What's blooming now is the clematis. This is the big, star-shaped one. They come in white and pink, and white with pink stripes, many other colors. They like lime, just a handful. It's a vine.

The cut flowers for the house come from here. I work hard to keep the colors complementary and avoid having blocks of color—rigid squares. It's common sense to put the tallest to the back, the hollyhocks and delphiniums, but you don't want them to appear too uniform, either. Get some variety in there. But plant at least five or six of any one thing so it doesn't get lost. And as a rule I don't mix the colors within a grouping. Oh, yes. And I treat them all like annuals. Even the perennials are discarded at year's end. Cow manure, peat moss and a sprinkle of 10-10-10. And a sprinkle of Epsom salts. That's what goes into this bed. I vary the flowers in this bed from year to year. For April blooms you might try salvia, phlox, shasta daisies, sweet william, daffodils, iris or daylilies.

Look close. Those scallop shells are holding the beer that catches the slugs. That's the organic way. Also, I get ladybugs from a supplier. You simply open the vial and loose them on your pests. I don't mind using Sevin dust, though. That will get rid of the snails and whatever's turning your azalea leaves to lace. Puts everything in its place. I'm no fan of marigolds. The smell will keep off the bugs, but my area's too small to fool with them.

On the opposite side of the garden, the parkinsonia is in bloom. Fine limbs like a willow but far less shaped. The leaf is about six inches long and a quarter inch wide. A fine-leafed tree—almost featherlike. They're all over Charleston. And the slightest breeze has them moving. Motion. Scent. Remember, there's more to a garden than pretty colors.

We're using concrete planters and urns throughout this section to create vignettes—to "paint" little pictures for the gallery. Junior clips the boxwood into perfect orbs to complement Mr. Briggs's circles. Now we slip past the reflecting pool, step up and then down, and enter Mr. Briggs's "natural" section. It's a circle of brick crowded in on all sides by a heavy, head-high planting of azaleas, hydrangeas, camellias, and much more. There's a different mood here under the big oak that shades this spot. It is borrowed from a neighbor, as is the one at the first seating area. The neighbors have the trunks and all the bother and I get the graceful limbs. I've been very, very lucky with my borrowed landscaping. You can see a big magnolia beyond the roofs, as well as the roofs themselves, and here across the back is a two-story wall of ancient, weathered brick. Be ruthless. If your neighbor has something pretty, borrow it from him. If it's not so pretty, you can plant it out of view or fence it out. If you're buying city property, keep all of this in mind. Remember what I said. Walk around and see what the possibilities are. A church steeple you would want to see but an aluminum-sided garage requires a shield.

But to return to this circle. It's been perfect lately for lunch parties. I've had Junior moving chairs about here. He says he's getting old and can't lift things. I don't mind getting old myself, but I don't want Junior getting old. He must stop right now. He will. Junior is even more optimistic than me. He's worked for professional landscapers. He's had a wealth of experience and he's plenty smart. He never loses his patience. I can't have him getting old. I just can't.

Well, it's so cool under the oak. I don't know what an oak exudes, but it's almost like air-conditioning. I've been told it's ozone but wonder if that's possible. Plus you have the grace-ful strength of those massive limbs and the rough texture of the gray bark. That's another fern growing along the tops of the limbs. Resurrection fern, for it droops brown and shriv-eled until the rain resurrects it fresh and green. And the Span-ish moss, such a familiar part of the Southern coastal scene we can forget to mention it. Those gray spirals are a way of fil-tering the air for nutrients. The moss is not a parasite, but I suppose everyone knows that these days.

The live oak forms a perfect canopy for this sunken garden, though the sink is actually only a single brick deep. The den-sity of the planting sets the mood. Keeps you encircled. And this spot doesn't depend on flowers. It's a lovely hot hole of color when the azaleas are blooming. Gorgeous, but only for those two weeks out of the year. What we have the rest of the time is a variety of leaves. Boxwoods. Hydrangeas. Ferns. A distinctive holly fern. And the camellias.

Camellias. You pronounce it ca-MAYL-ya. My birthday is on January 29 and very often that is about when they hold the camellia shows. My mother, Nan, would get up a big trip for my birthday when I was young. She would fill the car with blooms and make a wonderful picnic lunch and we'd take off. But I haven't been since. My garden doesn't produce a competitive camellia. I don't understand it. I've tried. In a show, you have arrangement classes as well as horticultural classes. You also have the gib class. If you gib your camellias in September they turn out a third bigger. And they bloom early too.

Gibbing. I don't believe I've explained that. Just a little drop of gibberellic acid where a bud's been popped off. Bigger blooms and earlier blooms. A way of lengthening the season. Of course, you sometimes try to lengthen more than the camellias. There are early-blooming bulbs—daffodils and

tulips. And some camellias bloom early without an assist. The debutante blooms in early November. A camellia that blooms too late has to compete with so much else. November, December, and January are the best months here. I've never been a judge, but you judge camellias by a lot of things. You want a distinguished bloom. The weight of its petal, the shape of the leaf, and the strength of the stem all factor in.

Camellias need to be pruned. A bird or a butterfly should be able to fly through the limbs. And azaleas need even harsher treatment. If you don't prune them on the outside they'll die on the inside. One well-known gardener nearby says, "Cut them back to the stump. That's the only way to prune an azalea!" He has a point, especially in a small garden like this. The azaleas can easily take over, and so can many other things. Don't be afraid to take them out completely. Take out a whole tree if you think it necessary. Make up your mind and do it. Also avoid the double azaleas, called hose-in-hose. When the bloom dies it hangs on the bush for days.

The hydrangeas in this circle are different from those at the entry. Shiny-leafed, and they bloom later. Remember, it's hydrangeas (and others) from the gate all the way back here, but they don't have to be identical. A dogwood gives you the bloom in the spring but also the texture of that gray bark. The sweet olive is evergreen. Both a shield and a fragrance. All of it closing in to a height of about ten feet.

And on the same central axis is another focal point. This one is a flowing fountain—one supplied by a hidden hose and pump. It looks like a mountain stream, but those rocks are not all that they appear. The biggest is a meteorite that fell in Berkeley County. Also, there's deep-sea coral, which the plants can grow straight through. And one of those smallest rocks was an unwanted bit of Roman ruin that my son-in-law Fred picked up in a parking lot while we were touring Europe.

Mr. Briggs didn't let his taste impinge on mine. He turned it over to me, so it's my fault for not doing more of my own earlier. I was in awe of him. But this little waterfall was my idea. There isn't a natural rock within a hundred miles of Charleston and complaints were made that my waterfall wasn't fitting for the area. I said, "Look here, Marty (Marty's my youngest daughter), this is my garden, isn't it?" Anyhow, I collect rocks and in that little waterfall is that meteorite that fell on Belvidere Plantation. It's sort of copper colored. Then, traveling with Fred and Anne, we came across a Roman amphitheater that had fallen down and that was being put back together in Switzerland. We pulled up to look and I slipped a little rock into my pocket. I got back in the car and Fred had a big one, and it's installed. Now I have rocks from Newberry County. Rocks from England, California, Flat Rock in North Carolina. Anyplace I see a rock, from the top of the world on down, I bring it back. Happy memories all of them, but it wasn't Briggs's idea.

There are more boxwoods behind the waterfall. Box is predictable. Small leaves and a cultivated form that suggests security. But we're getting to the edge of the wilderness again. A Hercules-club is volunteering—poking up among the loquat and sweet olive and domesticated ferns. The garden ends.

But wait. A little path leads off behind a bench. A path so narrow it usually has to be pointed out. Visitors often like this last part best of all. It's a little surprise. An adventure that beckons us in. We must turn sideways to enter.

This section is completely my own and was done after Mr. Briggs left. I have a personal chair back here hidden behind a large ligustrum stump, and at the opposite end, a good thirty feet away, is another flowing fountain and a terra-cotta fox. Just the fox and me peering at each other down a two-foot-wide corridor. To the right is the mellowed brick wall of my neighbor's ancient two-story carriage house. To the left is all the rest of Cheeka's endeavor.

The ligustrum trunk is a reminder of the original garden. It's big enough to hide behind and gives a nice rustic feel. Along the wall I have a high huckleberry bush and ferns and wax myrtle and bay and a faint whisper of Virginia creeper. Huckleberries were a treat in olden days, though I'm not keeping this bush for nourishment. And the wax myrtle is marvelous. An evergreen with a fine wax berry, and oh so hardy once it has its feet down. The bay is the sweet bay or laurel. It has petals like a miniature magnolia and the leaves are blue-green. This is my true wilderness. Over the years I brought this soil in from Berkeley County. I brought it in buckets. And then I transplanted the woods themselves. Most all of these plants are from Berkeley County. And the little fox keeping watch over this wild wood's fountain—he's a creature of those parts as well. And this fountain has a red rock that my youngest grandson brought from the Alps. Such good memories. One of these ferns is from the Golden Eagle, a motel and restaurant in Beaufort. I went there on a yacht with Ben. We went with our friends and I was given the fern by the motel owner. This lane is like a scrapbook. It's a place to invite your soul for a visit. That was Nan's phrase and it suits me. I sit here with coffee in the early morning or a drink in the late afternoon. At my feet is a statue of a cat about to pounce upon an unsuspecting statue of a bunny. My friend Patty is such a purist. She said, "Emily, you bought that concrete cat? What's wrong with you? I thought somebody gave it to you." I don't take my statues all that seriously. I try not to take myself all that seriously either.

I sometimes joke that this spot is my lovers' lane, the only fly in the ointment being there is no lover. It's just a lane plain and simple. I come here in the morning, still in my night-gown, to drink my coffee. I look down the way and see my rocky fountain and the little terra-cotta fox. My imagination goes on and on. A lot of the time I think this garden is complete and then I realize it could be better and the next day I'm starting over.

Remembering

Nan

GROWING UP IN PINOPOLIS, EACH OF US HAD A HORSE. PINOPOLIS TRANSLATES AS "city of pines," though with no more than three hundred residents, it could hardly be called a city. It's still there today, an hour's drive above Charleston. Still a small village with a main road—the Big Road—and lanes that lead off of that. The homes aren't too fancy—ordinary frame houses and cottages for the most part—because these little pineland communities were meant only for vacation living. In the beginning, people thought the pine trees somehow prevented the malaria fevers, and families came in from the plantations in May and stayed until the first hard frost. Even after they knew the mosquito caused the disease, the families still came in and they kept the pine trees growing because they were so majestic.

Pinopolis was situated in a forest of mature pines but close by was a true wilderness—untrampled beautiful countryside with streams, swamps, big pines, and all those unplanted fields. Sheer beauty is what my mother saw when she came down from Belvidere. Belvidere was the cotton plantation where she'd been raised up until the day of her marriage, which was April 14, 1910. When she married young Dr. Fishburne and came to live in this little pineland community, there was a horse waiting for her. Nan upset the village ladies. She would ride out our big gate, turn left, and ride a thousand yards to put herself on the edge of five or six thousand untrampled acres. Nothing was being planted. Lovely streams, incredible woods, a paradise for wildlife, a paradise for Nan. These swamps were filled with untouched cypress and tupelo gum, dogwood and holly. Nan rode every day. She had had a pony at the age of two and was an excellent horsewoman. But all this upset the village ladies because in the first place none of them rode horseback and in the second place Nan was pregnant almost immediately. Still she kept going riding and she went alone. Except for the hound dogs.

Nan said that when she and her new husband drove up to the house from Belvidere Plantation, which was twenty miles away, a hound dog got up from a pile of straw over here and bayed and another over there got up and bayed, too. None of them were kept in pens. They slept around the yard in what-ever soft spot they could find and Nan said when she and Dad got out of the buggy they were surrounded by hound dogs all wanting attention. Later Dad would say he couldn't have a dog of his own as long as Nan was here. They'd all desert him for her. Which was understandable. She never went outside with-out scraps for the dogs and a lump of sugar or half an apple for her horse. You could see why Dad didn't have a chance.

So each morning she'd get on that horse—a lovely dappled gray mare named Molly who, if the truth be known, was skit-tish, fractious, and hard to handle even for Nan—and with all the hounds following she'd be gone for at least a couple of hours. The crops had failed and the area was very, very sparsely settled back then. Cabins here and there. But per-fectly lovely streams and canals and Nan knew where all the masses of jessamine and violets grew. She knew where all the lilies grew. Oh, a spring swamp line, that row of fresh spring growth, is one of the most beautiful things in the woods. Such tender colors. Tiny little leaves. Willows. Maples. A swamp line in the spring is unbelievable. And those big deserted fields. It wasn't solid woods. Streams the color of sherry. Or they could be almost dry, showing lovely white sand. Then,

after a freshet, the water would be up to the horses' stomachs. I've ridden with her when the horses had to swim. Nan was a wonderful horsewoman. The horses knew they'd be getting a treat. She could put her fingers in her mouth and whistle and the horses would come up to her. She was wonderful with animals.

In those early days, Nan would get on her dappled gray mare after breakfast and go nobody knew where. If anything happened to her there would have been nobody around. But she just traveled until she knew every path and kept riding practically up to the day I was born. Mr. Bill Carson, a hunting friend of ours, used to say my mother knew the Wassmasaw Swamp like the floor of her bedroom. She had a great sense of direction and could tell where she was by the sun or the moon. She would start out the gate and every hound would leap up out of its bed of straw and take off after her. She'd be riding with the pointers and anywhere from five to ten hounds. They'd jump rabbits along the way.

All those animals lived in the lap of luxury. We had a married couple—James and Louisa—who lived in a house in the yard. James tended the horses and Louisa tended the dogs and cooked for them in a big black pot. That pot held ground corn and what Dad called "crackling"—bones and cured parts of various animals. That pot was huge and every dog had its own dish. So there was a circle of dogs around Louisa when she dipped from the pot. And on Saturday she had a barrel of whatever it was that killed ticks or anything else. Louisa would get James to help her dip every dog up to its neck.

Later in life, Nan had an automobile and she would keep a box of dog biscuits in it. She also had a book of poetry and a book on wild birds and wildflowers in there too, and when she died I said I had dibs on everything in that car. And I got it all.

The post office was across the road from us and when Nan drove there the village dogs would gather. They knew the sound of her car. By the time she got to the post office ten dogs would be waiting for the dog biscuits. At home, we had brick pavement at the foot of the front steps where she'd throw broken corn every morning. The redbirds learned to be there at a certain time and if she was late there'd be much chattering and carrying on. Nan was always prepared. Dogs to redbirds to people. She was persistent and accountable.

Dad had a special name for her. He called her Nancy. No one else called her that, but when Peach and I began to say a few words, we called her Nan—and Nan she was to us, to all her grandchildren, and to many of her friends. But to most in Berkeley County she was always Miss Anne. I never heard her call Dad by his first name, Kershaw. Dad was Doc to most people, but to her he was Sugar or Sug. That was her special calling name for him. They also called each other by whistling.

Nan was twenty-three when she came to Pinopolis from Belvidere Plantation. She loved the country life and needed that uncluttered space. She also needed a certain amount of time to herself. I never knew her to have a confidante and she seemed totally uninterested in gossip or idle talk. She enjoyed people, however, and was available to anyone needing a sounding board.

Her mother had taught her that the most important skill to acquire was self-discipline, and she had acquired it. I never heard her raise her voice, never heard her say the slightest derogatory word about anyone, and yet she was still a spontaneous person—immediately grieved, sympathetic, loving, or happy for others. She seemed to know instantly what was right and wrong. There seemed to be no gray areas. She wanted the best for everyone. She was always ready with a boost for everyone and she could soothe and calm any disruption amongst others. She used to say that she carried around a pitcher of oil to pour on troubled waters. Nan didn't avoid companionship, but still she needed that time alone to, as she phrased it, "invite her soul" or "catch up with herself." She wanted to sift and sort out her thoughts, to pursue her vision, to consider life.

My mother was pretty. She was five-foot-two and weighed between 125 and 130 all her life. She held herself erect and had a firm, fast walk until she reached her mid-eighties. She took a cold bath every morning until she was sixty-five, when her doctor made her switch to warm water. She loved Yardley's English Lavender and always put a drop of toilet water here or there. One of my many memories of Trinity Church in Pinopolis is when Nan would open her pocketbook and there inside would be her clean, lacy handkerchief with its lavender fragrance.

Her attendance at church was as regular as the seasons following one upon the other. Her faith in God, Jesus, and the Holy Spirit seemed to be her central motivation. She seemed to be guided completely by the teachings of Jesus. She was never late for church and followed every word of the service. She was ready with her offering and sang every syllable of every Venite, Jubilate, and hymn with reverence and gratitude. She discussed the sermon at the next family meal. If someone was absent from the congregation because of illness, some special delicate morsel would be sent over along with a magazine.

And on top of all this she enjoyed herself so. I take great pleasure in remembering how she enjoyed herself. She took delight in life and taught us never to wait for fun to turn up. She wanted us to go out and find it. Besides her riding, she played a good game of tennis and a respectable game of golf and enjoyed playing bridge, which she called mental calisthenics. She was in a bridge foursome right up to the end of her life. My mother never complained, but for health reasons she kept herself on a very strict diet. She didn't drink and didn't eat meat. She never said it, but she was a vegetarian. She lived to be ninety-four.

$\mathcal{D}ad$

$\mathcal{D}$AD CAME TO PINOPOLIS IN 1906. DR. CAINE HAD DIED AND OLD DR. WILSON called Dad, who borrowed a thousand dollars from Dr. Wilson and Dr. Kirk and bought a horse and buggy and cache of drugs. He got a room with Cousin Deas Porcher. In later years, Cousin Deas would come over to our house every day at milking time. She'd come with an empty pitcher and take it home full of fresh milk. I think Cousin Deas was dead in love with Dad. No doubt about that. Very few women crossed his path who weren't. He was just that attractive to women. He boarded with Cousin Deas for two or three years. Back then people were always wondering who Dad was in love with and there is a story Cousin Deas never lived down. The story went that Dad was asleep on the sofa in her parlor and she'd heard that if you put a sleeping man's hand in a bowl of warm water he'd tell the truth in his sleep. So here was Cousin Deas with a bowl asking him who he was in love with.

Dad woke up laughing and told the story all over the village. His laugh rang all through those pine trees.

Dad had this scattered rural population to look after and he was blessed on all sides. All of them, young and old, black and white, called him Doc. In area, Berkeley County is the largest county in the state and there was only one other doctor to cover all of it. Dad was always available. He'd go anywhere and if need be he'd sit up all night with his patients. He did everything from delivering babies and soothing the dying to pulling teeth and advising on marital and child-raising prob-

lems. People trusted his judgment and his horse sense. They trusted him because they knew he would do everything possible to assure their welfare. There was only one drawback. He kept this pack of hounds that sucked eggs all over Pinopolis, and howled too, but nobody would complain. They spoiled him so. Then came my mother.

Dad met Nan at the St. Cecilia ball in Charleston. She was pretty and petite. She was an expert horsewoman. She had traveled widely. And she'd grown up just twenty miles from Pinopolis and wanted to stay in the country. They suited each other perfectly, but my grandmother, who was running Belvidere by then—my grandmother Anne, of whom it was said, "She with the steel fist in the velvet glove"—she objected. They said my grandmother had only one fault: She thought no man was good enough for any of her three daughters. She had gone through terrible poverty. Her father had been killed in battle at Missionary Ridge. Then her husband, my grandfather, had a brain fever that almost killed him and left him with no short-term memory. So she'd been running the plantation herself and depending on relatives in the North for survival. She'd been through all that and didn't want it for her daughters. Having Dad, a poor country doctor, for a son-in-law didn't suit her at all. Furthermore, she thought that Dad had an eye for the women and that the women had an eye for him and that he wouldn't make a steady husband or ever make any money. Actually, she was pretty damn right about the whole thing.

What she did was write to her sister-in-law, my mother's Aunt Lizzie, who went abroad for five months every year. She traveled all over Europe in the grandest style and was always taking my mother and other relatives along. So my Grandmama Anne says, "Aunt Lizzie, I need to get my daughter out of town. I just don't like this doctor she's going with, so can't she join you on this next trip?" Nan was gone for five months, but when she got back and got off the train in Moncks Corner (which is next door to Pinopolis), there was Dad waiting at the bottom of the steps, with the whole town standing around. Nan just fell into his arms. That was the end of it. My grandmother was licked.

They were married in 1910 in the Belvidere garden—that lovely old garden with the irises and Louis Philip and Cherokee roses. The wedding was kept simple since Nan had gone against her mother's wishes by marrying Dad. When it was over, Dad and Nan left in a buggy with a runaway horse. Of course, Dad was just giving a runaway appearance. Giving a flourish. Every dog at Belvidere went after them—but the dogs gave up at the Belvidere gate when they realized it was going to be a long trip. Dad and Nan drove the twenty miles over to Pinopolis where he had bought the old summerhouse of the Ophir Plantation. When they got there, an adorable white kitten that my mother named Snow was waiting on the porch, and of course the dogs and Peter Heyward, the buggy boy, who rode with Dad when he was traveling around Hell Hole Swamp and the rest of Berkeley County.

Dad always had a buggy boy to tend the horse while he was inside delivering babies or easing someone into the grave. This was in the days of house calls and he often took along his gun and his pointers. If there was no emergency, he and the pointers would hunt one side of the road going and the other side coming home. Regardless of who owned the land. He just hunted where the sandy road wended its way. There were so many coveys of partridges, his dogs didn't have to leave the road more than twenty-five yards or so.

These pointers were the dogs he claimed Nan had stolen away from him. In medical school in Charleston his special pointer had come every day to one of the lectures. The dog had its own chair. Don't ask me how. Dad had personality coming out of every pore and could get people to agree to anything. In Pinopolis the pointers were allowed to stay in the house. They lay in front of the open fire. Best place in the house. Dad trained them. He never left the table without taking a tidbit. He would get down on the level with the pointers and call them. He'd hold a piece of meat within an inch of their noses and say *heed heed heed*. They'd better heed. When he said *hi on,* they could have the treat. There was a constant teaching of the pointers and they were beautifully trained.

The hounds weren't as favored and Dad finally had to pen them up because they were killing chickens and, as I've told you, sucking eggs all over Pinopolis. One night those penned-up hounds were making a racket. They'd be quiet and then start up again. Those twelve or fifteen hounds were making a racket. Dad had a bullwhip and he would crack it to make them stop barking. That night Dad went out on the porch in his nightshirt and his one eye and cracked the bullwhip and they got quiet. He got back in bed and snoozed off and the dogs started up again. He went outside again and quieted them. He did that about four times and he thought, What is doing this to these dogs? Then he heard a bark like a fox and

he finally realized it was Dwight Porcher who was doing it. Dwight would stand on his porch and bark like a fox, wait for Dad to get up and get the dogs quiet and get back in bed, then he'd bark again. That was a fox joke.

We foxhunted in the fall. This was after I'd completed my education at Ashley Hall in Charleston. As the sun rose we'd be up. Mr. Bill Carson would ride over on his horse with his three or four hounds. Dad would say, "Come on in, Bill," and the two of them would stand at what Bill called the wash-hand stand, which was the highboy sideboard. And they'd both pour up about half a glass of whatever they were drinking— generally corn liquor. They'd follow that with a couple of swallows of water. I went with them whenever I was at home. We'd start out in the dark, but just as daylight was turning up. We'd stay in the saddle until noon or one and end up God knows where. I always had the good luck to take out behind a man who knew what he was doing. I wasn't breaking the ground. Pure heaven. Because he had only one eye, Dad didn't ride hell-for-leather. Several men did—Johnny Hill was one—God he was fun to follow. Dad couldn't take those big chances. He had lost his eye before he married my mother. He liked to buy horses that had stamina, which very often meant they'd be strong-willed and difficult. One was particularly so and only Dad could shoe that horse. He had somebody hold it. Much ado. One day when he was shoeing it, a piece of steel flew off and got into his eye. They couldn't get it out for him in Charleston. They sent him to New York, where after ten days of intense pain the surgeons took out the eye and gave him a glass one.

Hunting was important for more than the sport. There was no set season for any game back then, which was just as well. We had no refrigeration. A shipment of ice would come up from Charleston occasionally, but there were no real grocery stores or meat markets or dairies in the entire county. You could buy flour, rice, grits, sugar, and lard by the barrel—or out of the barrel—in Moncks Corner. So people raised what they ate or hunted for it. Dad was a happy and avid provider.

He liked getting off with the men. They would hunt deer and fox. They would fish and drink liquor and talk politics and tell tales and play poker. But often I would hunt with him, and Nan did as well. Of course, Nan never fired a gun in her life and neither have I. We just went along.

Nan explained it to me. If, for instance, you're hunting quail and the birds flush, there aren't but one or two good opportunities to shoot. It is much better to let the man do the shooting and you stand behind him and do the complimenting. That's the attitude of a traditional wife, I guess it's safe to say.

Anyhow, Nan and Dad started married life together in the garden at Belvidere Plantation surrounded by dogs and in a runaway buggy. They came to Pinopolis, where he was practicing medicine. My grandmother Anne was right about there not being much money around. Hell Hole was what a lot of Berkeley County was called. It was wild in some places. In most places it was poor. A lot of the people had absolutely nothing and the main business was the illegal liquor business. Many of Dad's patients would pay him in venison and collards. Cash flow was definitely a problem.

In 1934 a change came about. Big changes with Roosevelt. The New Deal definitely changed Berkeley County for the better. Some of the money was misused just the way welfare can be misused today, simply because it involves human beings. My father left general practice at that time and became the county health officer. Maude Callum, a nurse, was as much responsible for his success as he was. She'd been trained as a midwife and as a public health worker and worked out of Dad's office, though she wasn't part of his staff. Dad was good at his job. Word got around. Dad and Maude worked together and did such a good job people came from all over —even India—to see how they ran Berkeley County's health department.

One time the telephone rang. Long ring, short ring. Dad's home for lunch. Nan says, "Sug, Hollywood is calling." Dad's quite deaf. He gets up from the table. Who is it? Who? Hollywood? She tells him it is Hollywood on the phone. Who? Hollywood, Sug. They want to talk to you. I don't have time for such carryings-on. Bang. He hangs up the phone. They'd read about him in *Life* magazine and wanted him to come to Hollywood. He thought that was ludicrous.

As I've said, my father was the most attractive man. He was all that a man needed to be. Six-foot-two with a vigorous laugh. I don't ever remember him being sick until he was in his seventies. He simply didn't succumb to such frailties of the body. He was strong mentally and physically and did everything. Played tennis and golf. But he had way too much sex appeal. Come to think of it, he might have done well in Hollywood.

Now, I should mention before going further that Nan's mother forgave Doc for abducting her daughter. Dad won not only Nan but eventually her mother as well and he was a source of pleasure and comfort to Anne Sinkler. He stayed in the Belvidere house the whole last week of her life and was beside her when she died. She was only fifty-four and had had a sad life. After his wife's death, my grandfather would live on at Belvidere for another fifteen years and my mother took on the long-distance responsibility for her father's care and the care of the plantation.

Dad and Nan shared the garden at our house in Pinopolis. It should have been thus, since they had fourteen acres surrounding the house. Quite a spread to tend. His interests were the camellias and roses and he joked that he didn't mind leaving the trashy perennials and annuals and the garden designing to Nan. I remember the careful preparation for every camellia show within driving distance. Trays were filled with Spanish moss and the blossoms selected. These were picked at the last moment and laid gently on the gray moss bed and eased into the backseat of the car. And off Nan and Dad would go. Such fun for them to have that mutual interest and anticipation and I remember the excitement of seeing their names in the Charleston *News and Courier*. They won ribbons and silver. That silver is amongst my most treasured possessions—the ice-tea spoons sit in one vase and the regular teaspoons in another.

During the camellia and rose seasons, Dad cut flowers every morning to take to the drugstore, hospital, and health department. I can see him there in the garden, on fresh dewy mornings, picking those lovely blooms. He thought of every plant as a child under his special care. When I remember all of this about Dad I wish we could have been contemporaries. We would have had so much in common and I would have enjoyed his personality. All that verve and intensity. All that enthusiasm. He gave his all to every interest. He put his heart, soul, and muscle into every single moment of life. But he found me to be an irritating teenager. Not as intense as he wanted me to be. I did not achieve star quality in areas he wanted me to—in short, I frustrated the hell out of him and he pretty much let me know it. As I grew older and, thank God, a modicum more mature, I too became intense about my interests. And enthusiastic about life. Now I understand his frustration entirely, but I took so long to mature that by then he was an old man and so we never met on an equal footing. We could have been pals. Too bad we missed each other almost entirely.

The Pinopolis Garden

MY MOTHER COULDN'T STAY OUT OF HER GARDEN. DAD SAID IF EVERY-thing Nan planted had taken, a rabbit couldn't have run across the yard. It was a blessing some of these things died. The place would have turned out to be a thicket. In later years when I visited Pinopolis, the first thing Nan and I did was the garden. I might not even go in the house first. I'd walk through the garden with her to see what was blooming, to see what was smelling delicious. She would show me this rose and that rose and what she was doing.

Nan enjoyed being outside, so she set about making it convenient and comfortable to be there. In that garden she had some chairs in the sun and others in the shade. In a secluded spot away from the house there was a fourteen-foot-square smooth concrete slab where she could set up her bridge table—either for a game of cards or for writing letters or for uninterrupted reading or for a session of reading aloud. That last activity, I loved especially. When her eyes began to fail she chose the books and articles and I did the reading and I could read for several hours with no strain on my voice. She was an expert listener and commentator and interested in a wide range of subjects—everything from politics and government to outstanding leaders and interesting people to gardening and art. Our ongoing education, you could call it. During the pauses would come the sound of the breeze flowing though the pine needles. Those mature pines—she called them her wind harps. The pine needles in the warm sun had a delicious smell. Nan deliberately enveloped herself in these sights,

sounds, and smells and just from accompanying her I learned to note the breeze touching my face and arms and to appreciate the way this same breeze moved through the foliage, fluid and alive. I began to truly see the amazing variety of shapes and colors of leaves and the part that the sky and clouds and sunlight and shadows played in the overall composition of both her garden and her life.

In their first year of marriage, Nan and Dad actually established two separate gardens. He planted vegetables and she designed their flower garden and began to collect rootings. Nan began her planting to the east of the house. She started very small and kept enlarging. First just a path with lots of flowering annuals. Then she branched out. She planted camellias in the shade of the big pines and soon she and Dad entered the camellia shows. She designed birdbaths and some more paths. She planted a magnolia tree, which to my mind is one of the worst things you can imagine. A magnolia tree takes up all the moisture so nothing grows under it, not even grass. But Nan loved hers and kept blossoms floating in the house. She started another garden with winter jessamine, flowering peach trees, and beyond these she had a rose garden—climbing roses on cedar posts with a summerhouse in the middle.

She had those old-fashioned roses. Louis Philip with its deep crimson color deeper fragrance. And she had Cherokees. I'm sure most of you know the Cherokee. A climbing rose, it blooms in the spring and the white bloom is offset by a dark evergreen foliage. A perfect rose except the blooming time is short. They've been around forever. They were brought from Europe and before that from China, I suppose. Very simple and absolutely Southern. If you see them in the wilderness they seem so in place, but you can bet they're on an old house site. Someone has lived within ten feet of that Cherokee rose. The Lady Banksia is another old-time favorite. Hardy. It takes little care. You don't have to spray it or do a thing. There are no thorns and it's more or less evergreen. Some years they are magnificent. Loaded down with cream-colored blooms. It's a small double bloom.

Nan rescued some locks from the Santee Canal, which was built hundreds of years ago to move freight between the rivers. She made seats from the locks. I don't know where they are now, but they weren't comfortable. Surrounding the rose arbor was a mass of violets blooming. So beautiful. I have some of those same violets in my garden today but they don't have enough sun. I also planted wild violets at the back of my garden. I put them around the little waterfall, but they've gotten lost. I should be nose to nose with wild violets and with the deer fern I put back there. That's a wild plant, too. It doesn't get more than six inches high and has a fine narrow leaf. I put forty little Easter lilies back there as well. I dug what we call "naked ladies" from the swamp and planted them all around the terra-cotta fox, but not a one is left. For the best. What Dad said about Nan's garden is true of mine. If everything I planted took, a rabbit couldn't find its way.

But back to Nan. As they'd done at Belvidere, she surrounded the roses with irises and she surrounded the irises with violets. Then more camellias were planted in the direction of the church. There was a ditch running from one side of the property to the other draining a little pond. She built a bridge across that and planted mountain laurel and anything else she could bring in along it. Cousin Deas and others used that path to go to church.

In those days there were no garden suppliers. Seeds were ordered from catalogues. You grew your own seedlings. Of course, Nan wasn't the only one gardening. As I said, back then everyone's garden was much like all the others in a radius of twenty miles or so because everyone had given everyone else a start of everything they took a fancy to. Louis Philip roses, hydrangeas, boxwood, syringa, bridal wreath, ferns, violets, banana and strawberry shrubs, and on and on.

Hydrangeas, I should mention, are particularly easy to root and make a nice Charleston or just plain Southern statement. Quite ornamental, with pink or white or blue flowers formed like lacy baby caps. Of course, they can get too big, which is the problem you have when you want to fit many of these larger "country" plants into a small city garden. At least the hydrangea gives you a large bloom. Elaeagnus doesn't. Nor does banana shrub. Banana shrub has this small bloom the size and shape of a pecan and the color of ivory. You hold the bloom in your hand and warm it. Smell and you get a double dose of banana. The bridal wreath that I mentioned is a spirea. What they sell for bridal wreath now is something else. In the old days it was a tiny white rosette of a bloom, but this modern one has a plume. I don't plant either type. The blooms just don't last long enough. It was said of the strawberry shrub that if it grew vigorously in a garden the wife ruled the roost in that family. I would not have wanted such a blatant statement in view in my own garden.

All these plants were shared with other gardeners and a

start could come in a variety of forms. Cuttings were rooted under the drip from the eaves of piazzas. There it was generally moist and shady. Also, everyone used plants from the surrounding woods and often shared these diggings as well. The woods, though legally owned by so and so, were there for all of us to use and enjoy. Gardeners "lived off the land."

Of course, the obvious advantage to these country gardens was size. The only vegetables I'm going to grow in Charleston are ornamental tomatoes. But out there they had room for everything. Fruit trees. Figs with those grand leaves and always bearing. Scuppernong grapes. I would hide myself in those arbors and eat until I was almost sick—or sometimes until I *was* sick. And as I mentioned before, they had room for those larger shrubs like elaeagnus, even if they weren't going to give a great deal in the way of bloom. And of course Nan had more room to experiment. She could put anything in the ground and then wait and see what happened. Wait years if necessary.

But Nan's Pinopolis garden is gone now. My Uncle Nick gave her a lovely brick wall. It wound through the oaks. Although the wall is still there, the fourteen acres of yard and fields have been subdivided. People are busy doing other things. The garden she had to the right of the house was completely plowed under. As I said before, a garden disappears unless you have a strong plan set in brick or someone who appreciates it. Then it remains. But if its design depends on plants that require care—plants that are tender and hard to grow—those can be overrun by the more vigorous ones, or shaded out. A garden requires nurturing. Time. Very few people have the time. Nan had a gardener five days a week, which brings me around to a last story.

I don't know if you know it, but there are two kinds of people in the world. One kind loves to prune and the other kind doesn't. Pinopolis sits on a high sand ridge and doesn't grow things easily. Nan was the kind who didn't prune. She said whatever the Lord would let grow she'd let grow. I *am* a pruner, and every now and then she'd have certain plants—vigorous plants that would take over—so I'd come up from Charleston and give her a day's pruning. She knew I loved it. She said, "Come early and I'll have Frank ready." Frank, who was her gardener, also loved pruning. When I arrived, there'd be two chairs set out and a long fishing cane. Everything in her possession that could cut would have been sharpened and assembled. And I was to point to where pruning would take place. Frank would be in good humor because he always wanted to prune and Nan wouldn't let him. He knew I thought he was a wonderful pruner, so he loved to see me come up. We would get started. Then Nan would say, "I want you to go on, but I can't stand to watch this. Lunch is at one." She'd go inside. Of course, Frank hated a woman directing him but could forgive me because I wasn't around on a regular basis. When Nan reached ninety-two she couldn't follow him anymore. Then he was an independent gardener for a while —until she bought a golf cart. When Frank saw that cart he looked like he'd sucked a lemon. Independence disappeared. Before Nan died she said, "I'm going to settle money on Cook and Frank when I die or you're to pay their wages til they die." We did the latter. Catherine, the cook, lived to be 104 and Frank died in 1991.

The Pinopolis Parlor

DAD AND NAN LIVED IN AN OLD SUM-
MERHOUSE FOR THE FIRST TWO YEARS
of their marriage. Then they were visited by
Aunt Lizzie. She didn't think the house up to snuff, so when
she got back to Philadelphia she sent a check for ten thousand
dollars and said build yourself a house. That couldn't happen
today. Not for ten thousand. Anyway, Dad knew a carpenter,
a Mr. Madson. Mr. Madson was delighted to come and build
a house.

Now, Pinopolis has this perfectly wonderful kind of dirt.
White sand on top. Just a thin skin on top and dark under-
neath. Nan said, "Mr. Madson, I want the house to look like
this." She scratched the first-floor plan in the dirt. "Give me a
wide, handsome front door. A large hall with two rooms on
each side. And the same arrangement on the second floor. Mr.
Madson, I have a picture of how I want the house to look." She

showed him a picture of a sort of antebellum Southern home. She said, "There are four columns in front with three windows spaced out between them." She said, "These are the kinds of steps I want. Is this all clear?" He said yes. She said, "I'm about to go to Pennsylvania for the summer. Do you need anything further?" No, ma'am.

I don't know where Dad was, but he was paying no attention. When Nan got back there was a tall narrow portico reaching over one window instead of three. And there were four of these huge columns all crowded together. Pillars. You had to practically turn sideways to get through to the front door. Mr. Madson, we can't get into the house. The pillars were square boxes with a little pointed roof resting on top. But Nan was never one to fight over anything like that, so they just took out two of the pillars.

Now, Aunt Em and Uncle Nick had many house parties at nearby Gippy Plantation and often one of the guests was an architect named Arthur Meigs. Nan would always invite Aunt Em and Uncle Nick and their guests to supper—coming to Pinopolis was an adventure for the Philadelphians. So the architect Arthur Meigs visited our house many times and eventually became good friends with my parents. One day he said, "Nan, I can't stand those pillars another minute. They grate on my nerves. They're so out of proportion. Do you mind if I give you two the right size?" Time went on. No pillars. Then one day up the middle of that sandy Big Road came a truck with pillars that reached halfway back to Moncks Corner. And they brought along a crew to put them up. That's where the pillars came from that are on the house today.

Odd-looking pillars weren't the kind of thing that concerned Nan. Especially not after the fact. The inside of the house was her concern. The first time she came to Pinopolis, Dad was living in spartan bachelor quarters. He'd been given a beautiful plantation-made, hand-carved double bed and an old desk with many pigeonholes. And here and there he had picked up a table and a few chairs. Nan took over the decorating. Except decorating wasn't a word in the Pinopolis vocabulary. Not at that time. Nan had curtains of blue chintz. Very pretty. Blue chintz in two shades, but they faded as they got older and older. She gathered us together in the hall one hot summer day and put up card tables. She took down the curtains and gave each of us a box of crayons. She said, "I want everything deepened two or three shades of blue." We did it with crayons. Then she put them back up. I remember that!

All of us. A bunch of children working over those curtains with blue crayons.

My house on Church Street. When I got here the parlor had no bookcases. Nan had bookcases in her parlor, so I put them everywhere I could in mine. I had been raised in a room that had ornaments—that had books and so forth. Nan had all kinds of things. A wonderful picture of Sam Porcher, a relative. I wonder where in the world that picture went? She had anything anybody had ever given her. A perfectly lovely decanter. Blue and white. Our friends the Brackets had given it to her. A red pigeon-glass decanter. All kinds of things. A photograph of a beau she'd had while traveling in Austria. He was dressed up in a uniform you wouldn't believe. Best-looking man, and I told that to somebody who said, "Your father let her keep that photograph?" He never made any objection.

Nan always had flowers in her house. The loveliest blooms from her garden. Four or five camellias or roses, sweet peas, violets or narcissus. She entered flower arrangements in shows, but the flowers in her house were always simple and unarranged. Her house smelled wonderful. She had roses through Thanksgiving and starting again in April. Another thing she used to do was for the linen closet—the sheets in those days were ironed. There was a material back then called voile, a very, very thin material that would allow scent to come out, and between the folded sheets she had lavender in bags of voile tied with satin ribbons. What a fragrance when you opened the linen cabinet. Linen sheets in those days. She had somebody to iron them. I wouldn't dream of having them now. Who'd iron them?

Nan sometimes kept a cotton plant in a silver pitcher. A racing pitcher. A trophy that was won in 1853 by a Sinkler

horse. There were two different Sinkler families. City Sinklers and country Sinklers. They all originally came from the same James Sinkler who settled on the Santee River and built Belvidere.

One thing we didn't want as children was for my mother to find us at loose ends. There were two or three things you'd be set to. You'd learn a piece of poetry, and it could be rather long. Or you could dust the parlor—that beautiful parlor I was describing to you. But from the point of view of dusting, it wasn't so lovely. I mean, every inch was jammed and you had to handle with care. Dusting the parlor was the worst thing. My roommate from Ashley Hall—Mary Hendricks—I just had a letter from her the other day. She reminded me of how much she loved a weekend at Pinopolis. Mary says Nan asked the two of us to dust the parlor and sat with us while we did it. Mary remembers Nan saying that really we should enjoy dusting that particular room since it was a privilege to handle the objects that were displayed there, all of them having interest and sentimental value for all members of our family. I never appreciated this angle—not then, not even when I was in my sixties. But that room will ever remain in my mind's eye as the most beautiful of all rooms.

It was painted a soft blue with a tiny tone toward gray. The ceiling was eleven feet high. To the east, between two windows, was a big open fireplace. And over it was a portrait of Nan's father and on either side of the portrait a handsome silver candelabra. To the south were two French doors opening onto an open brick piazza twelve feet above the ground and overlooking the formal portion of the garden and the lawn to the south. From there you could see the big pine trees and the Episcopal church. On the north side of the room was Nan's piano, which she'd brought with her as a bride from Belvidere, and this was flanked by two comfortable chairs. Above the piano was a narrow mirror and on the piano were two beautiful Dresden china candelabras. They were in the form of trees, each with a ladder resting against the trunk and on each ladder was a slender girl in a pastel dress holding a basket of tiny flowers. Up and down the trunk of the tree were leaves and roses and each girl wore a hat covered with tiny, delicate flowers. Between the candelabras was a Dresden bowl held up by four Cupids. And on the wall was a large engraving framed in gold of the victory of Constantine.

On the west side of the room was a small Victorian sofa inherited from the Belvidere parlor, and on this Nan kept her beloved scrapbooks. Some were about the horse races at Belvidere that she organized in the 1930s. Others were on gardening. Some simply contained beautiful scenes cut from magazines, scenes that had given her pleasure and that would spark her imagination for the rest of her life. Above the sofa hung an Italian mirror that had been inherited from Windy Hill Plantation, and on either side of this mirror were pictures of Dad's family — his mother and brothers and his sister. She hung this little gallery to let him know she valued his family, though through circumstances she could not control they saw little of them — one being that Dad and his father were not congenial and the other being that there were sixty miles of dismally bad road separating Pinopolis and Walterboro — rutted sandy stretches with muddy bogs in between. When we did set out for Walterboro, we took along a shovel and several planks. In the early 1920s no woman would dream of undertaking the trip without a man along.

On the left side of the hall door was Nan's desk, the one given to Dad by Cousin Deas before he was married. It was originally from Ophir Plantation and many years later I heard that some of the descendants of the Ophir family said that it should not have come to rest with us. I ignored the murmurings and Nan never knew of them. As with every other flat surface in the room, this desk held all sorts of inherited mementos—a brass-and-glass French clock, two delicate, clear Venetian glass wine decanters, a cream-colored footed and covered tureen with initials and decorations embossed in gold leaf—this from a famous set of china once owned by General Francis Marion's family. Above the desk was my favorite picture in the house—a large steel engraving of a girl leading a quiet cow.

Sitting and daydreaming at this desk with the French doors open was an experience I enjoyed. The fragrant aromas from the garden, especially those of the three large sweet olive trees that kept the house scented all winter, the soothing sound of the wind in the pines, a mockingbird or cardinal singing, the sounds from the village. Familiar voices or house dogs running after rabbits or baying. All so familiar, all caught in a moment of time. I thought it would always be the same, that it would never end.

In the center of the room was a round Empire table that held Nan's collection of garden and art books. In the center of the table, on a raised Chinese stand, was a silver pitcher won by our family's horses in the 1850s. It might be holding several stalks of cotton or bay blossoms, holly, camellia branches—anything.

Nan kept her radio in this room and she never missed the New York Philharmonic Orchestra. The condition of the world was also of unending interest to my mother. Before she came to breakfast, she listened to the radio and immediately after grace she would tell us what was going on in the nation and world. She was of a persevering nature and she was sometimes disappointed in her attempts to spur us on to an intelligent exchange of thought. But she guided us at every meal and, as I said, was proficient at handling buckets of oil to pour on troubled waters, often hastily diverting the trend of a conversation to avoid what might become an acrimonious dispute.

She also had those several simply-built bookcases. The one beside Dad's special chair held medical books. Poetry and novels were by Nan's sofa. She loved poetry, and at Cousin Anne Sinkler's school at Eutaw Plantation, memorizing poetry had been given much importance. Gray's "Elegy," much by Tennyson, Wordsworth, Longfellow. She could recite these poems up until she died. As I mentioned, in Nan's automobile when she died was a paperback book of poetry, along with that box of dog treats and the book on wildflowers and wild birds. I remember her efforts to have us memorize "The Village Blacksmith." At our summerhouse in Flat Rock, North Carolina, Nan and my aunt would often start reciting. You could tell they were homesick for the old times.

As for my own home—my own parlor—I can't think that anyone would ever consider it to be decorated. Not the way an interior decorator would do it anyway, but I do think it has a good feel. You know, a room that is not enjoyed, that doesn't have entertainments in it, a room like that becomes very cold, insensitive. Of course, the same applies to a garden. If a person doesn't live in a garden, think in a garden, create in a garden—well, it's the same as an insensitive house. In my own parlor I've created little groups. To one side is a table and three chairs. That's a conversational group. There's a sofa and two more chairs—another conversational group. In my parlor I play the piano, I have a drink, I sit by the fire. It's a fairly small room, but each activity gets its space. This makes the room warm and lived-in. Decorating, the kind Nan did and I try to do, is simply the result of a lot of use and happiness going on. In that room of mine, if I want a glass of sherry, it's right there. It's a lure for the guests. I'm casting out my fishing lines. The same rules go on in the garden. It can be totally unwelcoming if it's put together entirely by a designer and then not lived in.

I did have Mr. Briggs for the garden design. I was lucky there. But I have never used an interior decorator. For one thing, I have my youngest daughter, Marty. She has great gifts along that line. She was going to get a degree in decorating but got married instead. So I've had Marty lending me a hand. The colors inside my house, they're ones I like to live with. They're my colors. I told Marty I'm never going to keep Rosie off the chairs or sofas or anything else. I told her the material for the upholstery had to be fixed so it wouldn't look like Rosie had been on everything rolling around neck deep. If I take Rosie in the kitchen for a bath and then put her down, she flies to that parlor sofa to dry off.

The other thing is the sun. My parlor has the windows to give a room full of sun, an atmosphere of warmth. The gold gilt of the old picture frames, the gold tint of the fabrics, it adds to this atmosphere of warmth. Of course, I have a garden room too, a little room that looks out on the garden. I have my husband, Ben Scott, to thank for that. Ben used to say he was sick and tired of not having a room of his own. This was when the girls were teenagers. He said, "Every time I come in the house there's somebody kissing somebody in the parlor and I'm fed up with it." So I said, "The porch is rotted down, why don't we put a room back there?" So we did. It was his parlor. It was Daddy's parlor for about two weeks and then it became the suitors' suite and Ben was again relegated to his bedroom upstairs. And eventually it became my garden room and it's my favorite, for it has a large plate-glass window looking out over the entire length of the garden.

So those were my helpers with the decorating. My daughter Marty and my husband, Ben. But first and foremost, my mother, Nan. "Eyes that see, ears that hear, lips that speak." She was a wise woman. She was my confidante, my mentor, and my closest friend—but to this day whenever I see a room whose surfaces all are covered with mementos and photographs, I say a word of thanks that dusting is not my job.

$\mathscr{P}$*inopolis*
$\mathscr{M}$*emories*

OOUSIN CARRIE CAIN WAS AMAZING. SHE DID THREE THINGS TO MAKE MONEY. SHE planted fields of daffodils and sent them each morning from Moncks Corner on the train to the Ladies Exchange in Charleston. The second thing was accomplished in her attic. There she had sawhorses with planks across them and sheets of glass spread over with drying apricot purée. Cousin Carrie made apricot "leather." Boiled apricot was rolled out, dried, sugared, rolled up, and cut with a razor. She put it in boxes and sent it to Charleston, too. The third thing Cousin Carrie did to make money was to make bonnets for children, which, of course, were sent to Charleston on the train along with the apricot leather and the daffodils. With the money from the bonnets she bought a horse, which she called Bonnet.

Pinopolis before the flood. That was its heyday. I suppose people were giving up and things were changing even when I was a child, but we had a grand time growing up in the village. Of course, we would feel sad when our friends, like the Cains, went back to the plantations for the winter. As I mentioned, it was customary for the plantation families to come in for the hot months—to avoid the mosquito season—and the men would commute back and forth from the village to their plantations. In November, at the first frost, the plantation children would leave us. But they always came back in the spring.

In those days, an Episcopal church didn't change senior wardens. We had the same senior warden for fifty years. The men never came into the church when the service started. They stood outside always, a knot of six or eight who would come in just before the sermon. Nobody thought that strange —the men all standing outside talking about hunting or crops or whatever. All the church windows on one side looked out onto our yard. You could see our two cows and the garden. Perfectly wonderful. But that was a different church from the one that's there now. It's a pretty little building but it's not the same church. I won't go back up there to visit. Not since Hurricane Hugo.

But first there was the flood. That was in the early forties.

They took all that land around Pinopolis and flooded it to make a reservoir for an electrical power station. They came in and cut all the trees on the land around the village, all that wilderness that Nan had ridden through while she was expecting me. All that land that we'd hunted on. It surprised us, seeing that. We had thought we were living in flat country. You'd come upon a branch—a stream—and you'd go downhill, but it didn't occur to you that it was a real hill. Not until the trees were cut. It was a hill and there was Fanny Branch with water the color of sherry. On the left was Wassmasaw Swamp and to right was Broughton Hall Swamp. That was a deep one, so deep they made a lake from it. To the left of us was Wassmasaw, where the horses had sloshed in water and around the hummocks, the round areas of trees all thick with wildflowers. And the birds. Unending coveys of birds. All that underwater now. After the flood, Pinopolis was a peninsula.

But in the village the tremendous pines still grew. They towered above us and the Big Road was lined with crepe myrtles. Nan did that. She organized the Civic League and came up with projects to make money. She wanted both Pinopolis and neighboring Moncks Corner to have civic pride, to have trees planted and trash picked up, and she nearly died when every standing tree on the Moncks Corner main street was cut down. Some things can't be changed, but she said nothing could be accomplished without perseverance. She persevered to the point where the mayor of Moncks Corner and a few others learned that it saved time to go along with her from the start, since they'd just lose the battle later on anyway. They'd say, "Here's Miss Anne coming. Whatever it is she wants, let's try and help her now."

I remember several after-supper meetings in our parlor that were attended only by men. She served blackberry wine and cookies. Two particularly successful endeavors were started that way, with blackberry wine and cookies in Nan's parlor. The horse races at Belvidere Plantation were the first one. The country up there is rich in limestone and all that calcium in the water makes it good for raising horses. Nan was running Belvidere by then and the young man helping her was raising horses on his own plantation. She thought his neighbors could do the same and the area might enjoy the kind of prosperity they had around Camden. So she built a track at Belvidere and the races were very well attended, though nothing came of the horse breeding.

The second of her blackberry-wine-in-the-parlor plans was

for the lancing tournaments at Gippy Plantation. Lancing was an old, old tradition they were trying to keep alive. It's a gentle form of jousting. It's tilting. A mounted rider charges at a ring with a spear. "Charge, Sir Knight" is the call to arms and each knight has a lady love whom he's attempting to honor. With the money Nan made from the lancing tournaments she bought azaleas for every yard in Pinopolis.

She also organized and chaperoned a dance every Saturday night for years at a vacant furniture store in Moncks Corner. That money was initially to be used to build a TB shack for quarantine in Berkeley County. She finally raised seven thousand dollars, which became the seed money for the Berkeley County hospital. And at her instigation, the Civic League turned into the Garden Club. She started the Book Club and was a faithful member of the Library Board. In later years when I went to visit, I'd say, "Skip your club meeting and come with me." She'd say, "No, when you put your foot to the fire you put it there." She was accountable and she loved to be doing, to have her projects. She wanted her community to look the best and be the best it possibly could be. Civic pride is just that. Being proud of what you have and wanting to share it with others.

Nan had ice cream churned and sold it under the oaks. She assembled a cookbook. She made money in all sorts of ways to pay a local man, Henry Thomson, to grub the underbrush and weeds from the abandoned places around the village. She planted the entire Big Road with dogwoods and crepe myrtles. They're still there, but the big pines are gone from Pinopolis. In 1989, Hurricane Hugo snapped off nearly every one.

But I've wandered far from the topic I meant to tell you about: Christmas in Pinopolis with the Cains. Their family did not celebrate on Christmas Day. That was a day of worship. But on the day after, their family came up from Charleston and different places to gather at Summerset Plantation. The three Dwight children would be there, too. And Peach and I would be there. We would walk or ride in the buggy. Spend the afternoon swinging on oak branches and having fun. Then we'd have a two-o'clock dinner. We ate in the big dining room, with all the grown-ups at the big table and the children at small round tables. After dinner the living room was closed off. The children were sent out to play in the yard and the men would go out and cut down a Christmas tree and put it up in the living room. The women would take candles in tin holders and dress the tree—nothing store-bought. It

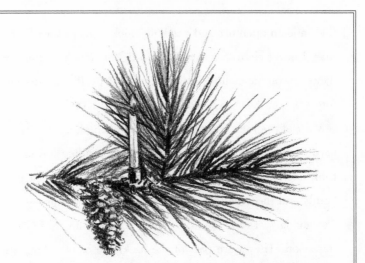

always looked lovely, though it was utterly and absolutely dangerous, of course. If the tree had caught fire it would have been the end of the house. Anyway, after the candles were lit the children were invited in and served tea and thin pastries and there was such laughter and joy in being together. It would be dark by then. We would dance around the tree and sing, "Christmas tree, Christmas tree, what have you brought for me?" Every single soul received a present. Then the children would play hide-and-seek in the dark while the adults sat around the fire. There was also a banister we loved—a mahogany rail to slide down in the big hall. Perfectly wonderful. We were put to bed in two big rooms with mattresses on the

floor and an open fire and a ticking clock. Except for Christmas, I never slept in a room with a ticking clock. Light was flickering on the ceiling, but you know I slept. If you were put into a bed in those days, you slept.

Most of the local plantations weren't planted, so they were hardly a source of income. When old Dr. Cain died, my father took over his practice. There were twelve children in that family and those children became all kinds of things—doctors and lawyers and the like. Cousin Carrie and Cousin Kitty stayed on. They were part of the backbone of the Women's Auxiliary and wonderful to the children in the neighborhood. Their summerhouse was always open to children. All the houses were. You would get the simplest of suppers and then play word games on the porch. It was all such fun. All of it.

$\mathcal{S}chool$

WHEN I WAS TWELVE I WAS SENT OFF TO ASHLEY HALL, A GIRLS' boarding school in Charleston. In Pinopolis I'd been attending a four-room school taught by four teachers. Each room had three classes. Whoever was sitting at the front desk was being instructed by the teacher. Then the next in line would move up to be taught. A great variety of ages were in that Pinopolis school. All were white and I remember a fourteen-year-old boy in the first grade. Ben Scott had a similar experience on Edisto Island.

Now Ashley Hall. I don't have any idea why I couldn't learn. Most everyone else could. But I was at the bottom of every class. It was hideous. My self-esteem suffered terribly. When you can't do well at school you think it's better not to try. If you're going to be defeated anyway, don't try. At least that was the attitude I took.

When I got to Ashley Hall I could do two things well: I

could play bridge and I could play the piano. I was also fairly athletic. My mother started teaching me piano when I was six. She was determined. Had she been any less determined she never would have gotten me to play. She thought I had a nice touch and she persevered until a music teacher finally turned up in Pinopolis. Alma Hudson. Nan said thank God for this and turned me over to her. When I got to Ashley Hall, Madame Begay took me over. She was a tiny Frenchwoman who never lost her temper. I played with her the whole time I was there. Then I played with Miss Finger. Nan thought I had possibilities and if I'd had her determination and concern with details I might have been able to play to some degree. Still, I did a lot of practicing. When I got married I had no piano for three years. Not good. You need to play continually. When we moved to Charleston Nan brought me the piano from Belvidere, but classical music takes two to three hours a day of practice. I mean if it's worth doing. That's not what I wanted to put my time to. I've played lots of music. The kind to dance to or sing to. All of the things that are part of everyday life. That's what I play.

But Ashley Hall again. My mother sent me off, away from Pinopolis and the four-room schoolhouse. I think I was very immature. Nan thought boarding school would be the answer. She didn't have the money, so Aunt Em sent me. And when I went, at age twelve, this is what my mother sent me knowing: I played a good game of bridge; I was good enough at sports to become number one on the tennis team at Ashley Hall and to join the swimming team, the track team, and the basketball team; and I played the piano well enough to play for dancing after supper. I danced well, too. No matter of anybody having to teach me to dance.

I played "Who" on the piano.

> *Who?*
> *Who stole my heart away?*
> *Who made me dream all day?*

I played "It Had To Be You" and "There'll Be Some Changes Made." All kinds of things I played. Nan had turned the screws down on me. It was a terrible shock to her that nobody could turn them down any further. I could not do one thing academically. But I could play bridge and do sports and I'd sneak downstairs and play the piano.

There were thirty of us boarding. I was the youngest. Two hundred and fifty young women, day students from Charleston and boarders from everywhere. I had a Canadian room-mate. I had a roommate from New Orleans. I was utterly ter-rified of boys. I was 5 feet 8¾ inches when I went to Ashley Hall at twelve years old. I weighed 120 pounds. I must have looked like I was hung together with safety pins. I didn't have a date until I was eighteen. I had the worst inferiority com-plex you can imagine. I felt as though I'd come from the banks of the Wassmasaw Swamp, which is exactly what I'd done. Yet I'd been taught good table manners. All kinds of things. But it didn't seem to matter.

French! They finally had to take me out of French. The French teacher, she would not give an inch. I wasn't learning the first thing. I don't know what. I think I drew. I looked somewhere else. I just couldn't understand one thing. So they finally put me over with Miss Baker. She was American and she tried to teach me French. I could finally read the French, but I couldn't pass the course. A disaster. My academic career left me feeling that I was a total failure. They sent my younger sister, Peach, there, too. Of course, she could answer every question they could ask at Ashley Hall, which only made it worse.

Math! I want to tell you this about math. When it got to

fractions I stopped cold. I made forty on a major exam in geometry. I was constantly at summer school. Terrible situation and there was my sister, smart as she could be.

I think schooling is a disaster for many children today. I don't think instructors get across to a child at that age that what they're teaching is self-control—control of the mind. It's got nothing to do with whether a subject is interesting or not. I was pretty good at history. Not bad at English. But parts of participles and stuff like that—that did not go in. I read a tremendous amount, but I didn't understand the purpose of the rest. I do now. You have a muscle here between the ears. When you play tennis, when you do exercises, you use muscles. The muscle up top is the same. Unless it's used it is going to be flabby. Those lessons are what develop it. That's why I learn new music all the time. Even now, even at this point, I want the exercise.

But not back then. At Ashley Hall, Miss Susan Mazyck was trying to teach me Latin, but after Christmas she wrote home to my mother: "Dear Mrs. Fishburne, Emily is a darling child, but she's not going to learn Latin. Next door to me Miss Jervey has a sewing class and I advise you to put her into that class." Academics! In a class of twenty I was twentieth. I was never eighteenth or nineteenth. I was always twentieth. Rock bottom. Four classes a day. But sewing. Now I *could* sew. A wise choice. That was fun. But they sent me out of Ashley Hall totally lacking in confidence.

Nan did explore every possibility that might make me self-supporting. I think she'd looked me over pretty carefully after Miss Mazyck's letter and realized that my academic skills probably were not going to be viable. She must also have noticed that most girls who were being squired around at that time were five-foot-two with eyes of blue, while she had on her hands a five-foot-nine rail of a girl overwhelmed by shyness.

She had already taught me how to play the piano, to ride horseback, to play tennis, to dance, to play bridge, but my mirror didn't help. When I looked in it, I saw eyes the size of saucers and full of doubt. The fact that I could do all the things she'd taught me better than most other girls didn't seem to count for anything with me. Even though I appeared to be popular with the girls at school, that didn't seem to mean anything to me either. I couldn't do academics and boys couldn't see me.

She didn't give up. She was the most persevering and determined human being I ever met in all of my long life. I never left her presence that she didn't tell me how much pleasure I brought into her life, how proud she was of me, and how good-looking and sweet I was. I wish I could say that I opened myself up and let her fill in all the chinks that were quavering and empty, but I simply found what she told me too hard to believe. Boys didn't see me and what I saw in my mirror cast doubt over all the stuff she was telling me.

None of my negative behavior deterred her for a minute, however. She went right to work and planned some positive moves for me, regardless of what I thought or said. She just quietly and steadily pushed forward. She thought one of the things I did best was play the piano. She knew that I wasn't concert quality, but she decided I'd be able to teach children to play, so she sent me to the University of Georgia to get a teacher's certificate and, indeed, I brought home the bacon. What a treat it must have been to see the satisfaction in our two faces. I wish someone had had a camera to record it.

Well, in the end, much to my surprise but probably not to hers, I finally began to jell. I put on some weight and filled out here and there. The boys began to see me! What an utterly delightful experience! I was off and running! Boys liked me! I was part of the crowd! What a blessed thing to have this cloud dissipate. I finally evolved into a somewhat viable human being. But let me say right here: The journey from birth to eighteen is no joke.

But learning and school. I'm not certain how these actually connect to the creative process. I mean, you have to say to yourself, Now pull up a chair. Then you say, Sit down. You ask yourself, Are you comfortable? You get yourself a cushion and then strike the first blow. If you're a painter, you take up the brush, dip it into the paint, and put it on the canvas and get going. Once you begin, it's divine.

Perhaps that's it. Can I do this? Perhaps creativity is linked to doubt. I have always had the strongest urges. I remember as a young girl sitting on the porch at Flat Rock and thinking, I've got to make something. Make something. Clothes especially. If I can't get to a machine I'll stitch a dress by hand. I've always sewn all my clothes. This is the first time in years I don't have a dress in the making. I love to sew. Love to cook. It's creative. Back then, when I couldn't do my Latin and Miss Mazyck put me in the sewing class, well, I had already sewed for my dolls by the hour and loved it. By the time I got grown and my children had dolls and they'd be sick—well, I'd make every kind of thing for every child and spread it all on the bed.

I didn't realize at the time that I was doing the part that was fun. If the children could have made the doll clothes themselves it would have been so much better. Which, of course, is what we had done as children. All of us made doll clothes. We had these dolls called Kewpies and we dressed those Kewpies. We'd sit around in the strangest places. I remember in Pinopolis sitting on the second floor of the back shed with doll clothes spread all around me. Making them.

Ashley Hall is where I learned about patterns. I can also embroider. Only thing I loathe to do is darn. I got out of that early. I knew how to do it when I got married, how to darn socks. I took the greatest care. Everybody was poor. You didn't throw away a pair of socks when one had a hole. My mother, if she got a run in a stocking she'd just stitch it up. She had the most extraordinary stockings, with all the runs stitched. I can remember Ben complaining about my darning and I said, "Look, they really hurt you? That's the best goddamn news I ever heard in my life." I said, "That's the end of darning. I'm so glad you're making some money. Whenever you get a holey sock, throw it in the trash and go get some more."

I've never darned from that day to this.

Twenty years ago, I came across a dress pattern that seemed

to me to answer all my needs: no zipper, no waistline, no tucks, four different necklines, and a full skirt. The pattern has paid off. I've made the dress for winter, for summer, for cooking, for gardening, for tea partying, and for dancing, varying the material according to the season or occupation. It has saved me oodles and oodles of money, which I spend more than happily in the garden. I have continued sewing this pattern year after year and I guess I seemed so pleased with myself that no one had the heart or nerve to tell me that enough was enough. Stop! Stop now!

No one, that is, until a close friend staying with me after Hurricane Hugo said, "Look, what is it about this blue dress you wear all the time? I'm sick of it."

I was, I can tell you, pretty taken aback. "What the hell are you talking about, Mary?" I said. "That's my favorite dress and I never once put it on that I'm not told how becoming it is on me. The color is perfect with my eyes and it's good in any weather and the most comfortable dress. That wonderful stretch material."

"All I know," Mary answered me back, "is I'm damned well sick of it. Why don't you buy yourself some good-looking, up-to-date clothes? You've got plenty of money!"

That wasn't the end of the matter, either. A day or so later I was packing to go to London and my eldest daughter, Miss Em, came over to make sure she was satisfied that her mother had the proper clothes for all possible occasions and weathers. She came bustling in to oversee every item and found the blue dress laid out suspiciously close to the hub of operations. Miss Em gave me the same sort of orders as my friend Mary had. And I answered with the same obstinacy. After all, I'm not trying to catch a husband. I merely want to look fairly pretty and want very much to be comfortable.

A year after the blue dress went to London with me, I was in Flat Rock, down on the lawn by the lake overseeing some planting in the picking garden. There was a call from a man out on the lake in a canoe obviously trying to catch my attention. "What did he say?" I asked my helper. My helper claimed that what the man in the canoe said was: You've got on that damned blue dress again.

The dress is still in use. Mary has put on her wings now, so she doesn't have to be consulted, but I am more restrained in my choice of days to wear it.

You know, in Pinopolis a person didn't have a coat to go with a pink dress and a coat to go with a black dress. You didn't have a party coat. You had a coat and were damn lucky to have a coat and nobody thought of buying a new one. You had a coat for years. The first new coat I ever had in my life my Aunt Em gave me for my trousseau. I'd been wearing the same one since I was twelve and it wasn't new even then.

I remember Cousin Lizzie wearing one of those old coats. All of them were the most rusty-looking things you ever saw in your life. One of the picnics we'd always do was Strawberry Sunday. Strawberry Church was the little chapel of ease ten miles down the Cooper River. There'd been a town there once and a graveyard that was famous because the cruel schoolmaster had tied little Miss Chicken to a tombstone there. But nothing was left of the failed town except for the church, which had services once or twice a year. We'd fix a picnic lunch and go down to Strawberry. One year it turned out to be a hot day for winter and Cousin Lizzie lay her coat down over a tombstone. When she came out after the service it was cooler, so she picked up the coat to slip it on and lizards ran out of each sleeve, the neck, everywhere. But I remember most of all how rusty-looking that coat was. It should have been black but it was used down to rust.

Nan was worse. She never bought clothes. When I got

completely sick of the clothes I'd made and figured nobody would wear them, Nan would say, "I'd like to have that when you get through with it." She and Aunt Laura wore my clothes for years. I had to send those old clothes off to the Goodwill to keep them away from those two. They would take my clothes and do them over. The clothes would come out looking better than when I first made them for myself. Neither one spent a dime on their backs. We had a terrible time making Nan buy a dress for my first girl's wedding. That dress sufficed for every wedding thereafter and it was a perfectly hideous dress. Lace of the most disgusting aqua color and shoes to match. That wedding was over at the little Trinity Church in Pinopolis. Nan came in the house immediately after the wedding and took off her shoes. The reception was in the garden. She had on the most mangy pair of shoes she had bought at Barron's department store (anything that cost more than twelve dollars and fifty cents was an absolute no-no). And hats! She kept them in boxes for decades and I know the youngest was fifteen years old. Anyway, she still always looked very attractive. Very clean and dainty. You always believed when you saw my mother that she smelled delicious. She was dainty.

As long as I'm on the subject of schooling and learning and creativity, I should mention painting. Gardening is simply doing pictures with plants and I think learning to paint has helped me there. Especially when working with small spaces — small gardens, and vignettes within larger ones. I mean, with plants it's like walking through an outdoor art gallery.

I didn't start painting until fairly late. I was out of Ashley Hall and back in Pinopolis. There was a wedding in Walterboro and the entire family was going. I was staying behind with a cold and Nan said, "Here are some oil paints. You can paint some pictures on drinking glasses. Copy this picture of ducks." Well, I soon realized I could copy anything. I did turkeys and ducks. I realized I could copy from nature. I must have been twenty. I played around with painting. Did five or six pictures a year until the family persuaded me to take lessons and I went and took lessons from an instructor. He discouraged me from the whole thing. I didn't pick up a brush for five years. He wrecked me. Now, however, when I travel with my daughter Anne and her husband I carry watercolors, and I'll keep a painting going in the garden room in Charleston and I'll paint at Flat Rock. I can't help it. I have a yen to create. You can create in cooking or gardening and it all overlaps. I don't have the perseverance the way my youngest daughter, Marty, does. She's the professional artist, the one with the courage and willpower. I've been a traditional wife and I've always defined "traditional wife" as a woman who puts down whatever she is doing to go to the place she is needed. *Then* you can go back and entertain yourself. It has certainly made for a very nice life, to garden, to play the piano, to paint as I do, to cook—but for God's sake, don't give me the cleanup.

Tennis

Y FATHER SAW THE CLAY. THEY WERE DRAINING THE MAIN PINOP-olis road and the new ditch had cut through a clay bank. Dad sent his one-horse wagon with James and brought in every bit that was dug up and built a tennis court in our yard. Actually, he built two courts in Pinopolis and Nan built a third. When Dad came home for lunch, he'd always stop to check on the court and set James to improving it. This is the same James who plowed our acreage and grew the corn for the horses, the James who had such a beautiful voice. On a spring afternoon when he was plowing, he would lay back his head and open his mouth and sing the most magnificent songs you ever heard. We could hear him all over the village. I mean full voice. Such an amazing voice. I remember him this way, and I remember him with Dad's homemade concrete roller pressing that clay court.

First Dad built the court and then he learned to play. Then

he and Nan taught their daughters and their daughters' friends to play. I did the same. I taught Miss Em, Anne, and Marty and their friends to play. You can't teach one person how to play tennis. It definitely takes two — or more. I took those young people around the state and put on a tournament for each age group. The cost of a silver teaspoon back then was only eight dollars and it brought such pleasure to the person who won it. I chose a pattern that would go with everything else — Fiddle Thread — and had the spoons engraved. The runner-up got a coffee spoon — a demitasse.

I know I must stick to the subject, but thinking about tennis reminds me of Cousin Annie Ravenel, who came to live in Pinopolis in 1950. She was elderly by then and retired from having run a very popular pension in Tryon, North Carolina, for many years. She chose Pinopolis for her retirement years because, as she became older, her steps and her heart began to turn toward the Low Country of South Carolina where she'd been born and brought up on a rice plantation south of Charleston. The plantation had been sold long since and her intimate family had scattered. There was, however, a coterie of cousins and friends in Pinopolis, so she rented a house there — a stone's throw from the church and in calling dis-

tance of my sister's tennis court. This spot was heavily traveled by children—my children included, for when they were
young, we spent every weekend with my parents. Cousin
Annie, who had lived a rich, varied, and very independent life
for an unmarried lady of her generation, loved children. She
soon let them know that she'd love them to stop in for visits
and that her cookie jar was always full of the most delectable
cookies called jumbles. She learned the ways of each child and
they learned hers. They often played card games with her.
They became intimates.

One Sunday during morning service, there was a commo-
tion up near the pulpit and everyone gathered around Cousin
Annie who had had a fainting spell. They laid her out on the
pew. As she came to and opened her eyes, there was a little
girl's anxious face peering down into hers. Cousie Annie said,
"Daughter, run quick and get my whiskey." The little girl, my
niece Moonie, set out at full speed and was back before you
could say Jack Robinson. Cousin Annie took a long swig from
her flask and in a moment, to everyone's relief, she sat up and
said, "I'll be fine now."

The reason Moonie knew where to find the whiskey was
that Cousin Annie's bedside table drawer was where she kept

only three things—her Bible, a deck of cards, and her flask. From then on, whenever she needed to be taken to the hospital, everyone knew those were the first three things that had to go into her bag.

And now back to tennis proper. When Ben and I moved to Charleston, I was appalled by the lack of community courts. It was pure brass on my part, but with only three courts on the whole peninsula, and these doubling as basketball courts and playgrounds, I felt something had to be done. I approached the head of parks and recreation, an old resident, but that plea fell on deaf ears. Next I approached two private

citizens about donating their yards, the way it would have been done in Pinopolis. The property owners were polite but they thought I'd lost my mind. I gave up and did my teaching on private courts.

I remember Marty's group in particular wanted to do anything but learn tennis, and my vocabulary has never been tamped down by living in the city. I was frustrated. That's my excuse. At a party later, a person who lived across the wall said, "My, Emily, you certainly were doing some double teaching over there. Tennis and profanity at the same time." Oh, but it is so frustrating to teach tennis to ten children who don't want to learn. A lot of children are very uncoordinated. Shannon was one and Poppo was another. Anyway, I taught them all the rules, who does what, and then I taught them each to hit the ball. How you move your feet. That's what matters. How you move your weight has a great deal to do with both tennis and golf. You have to follow through with your body weight exactly right.

Being raised in the country we made our own fun. We danced on dates and carried on conversations and we played lots of bridge. A party was a bridge party. I can't remember when I couldn't play bridge. Nan taught us immediately.

Knowing your partner and agreeing on a set of rules between yourselves is the key. I played with Ben two or three times a week. He'd learned young. When it got too hot in the middle of the day, we sat down and played bridge. We had bridge instead of air-conditioning. Nan said never stop playing, it's mental calisthenics. You learn how to add and subtract in a very minor fashion and if nothing else that lets you take charge of your purse.

I play on Mondays with three women. We don't play for money. We never played for money in the country. When we play bridge, we're spending time, and time is just as valuable as money. More so. I've found that lying down or taking a nap or just sitting in a chair is often not the answer to being tired. Just change what you're doing and that can be the same as drinking a Classic Coke. The weariness diffuses and slips away. I skip the nap and play the piano for one hour intensely and when I quit I'm fresh. Or I go out in the garden. Just change what you're doing—your mind gets involved and you're refreshed.

"Sixty-Minute-Man." That song has such a wonderful rhythm for dancing the lindy. We used it to teach the lindy and I played it hell-for-leather. And of course I had no idea what the lyrics were about. Not the remotest idea what was being sung. And of course all the young dance students understood the song, which is still wonderful to dance to and I still do play it. We used to teach them with the old song "Alley Cat" as well, which is probably just as bad and just as much fun to play. I can get so wound up playing.

So much modern dancing that I see on TV is just sexual display and has nothing to do with what we taught, which was the lindy, where you touch hands but you're moving separately to the same rhythm. We also taught the waltz and the fox-trot, as well as the cha-cha and the rumba and the tango and several line dances, which are coming back now. We also taught square dancing. I was the caller and very good at it because you need a voice that carries—a voice that doesn't tire. You have to control a room full of people and you can't if they can't hear you.

The hardest part of teaching dancing is confronting someone who has no sense of rhythm. You can teach people every step on earth but if they aren't moving to the music they simply can't dance. Step, slide, close, step, slide, turn. You can get the whole damn thing down but if you can't move to the music you can't dance. And the worst part is, a person without rhythm doesn't know he can't dance. Let me say something in your ear, I tell them. You aren't keeping time. You're going up and I'm going down.

At my granddaughter Emily's debut we had a perfectly grand orchestra. I needed a partner and asked an old friend who was a wonderful touch on the piano. I asked him, "Can you dance?" and he said, "Yes, I can dance. I did very well at the debutante parties in Philadelphia." I decided to take a chance with him rather than a not-quite-so-attractive man who happened to move perfectly. What a terrible mistake. As a dancer, that wonderful pianist had no more connection with the music than my dog has with a hot-air balloon. Anyway, I'm getting a bit nervous these days, for I've reached that stage in life when I might stumble a bit. But with a man who is steady and has a good sense of rhythm, I still love to dance— pure delight!

But teaching all this to the young was probably the best fun of all. You don't know how your daughters will end up or where, but social skills can certainly help them land on their feet. Playing bridge or tennis or knowing how to dance or ride will help them make friends wherever they are. My three daughters all ended up with careers but they still do these things well. They may never need them but a time might come. I expect it's better to have and not need than vice versa.

And lest we forget, I'll repeat that time is money. It's like money, anyway. If you have a hundred dollars you have to figure out where you want to spend it. Exactly the same with time. You know there's nothing worse than flat-out boredom. Sometimes I think bad feelings are better than no feelings at all. At least bad feelings have movement to them.

Living

$\mathcal{B}$ e n

I MARRIED BEN SCOTT WHALEY IN 1934. HE WAS CLERKING FOR SENATOR JAMES Byrnes in Washington, D.C. Ben Scott had a law degree from the University of South Carolina. While in Law school, he'd served a term in the state house of representatives and had been reelected. He was an associate at a Charleston firm, which is where Byrnes had recruited him from. Ben knew South Carolina and he knew all kinds of people. When Congress was out, we'd leave Washington and live in Spartanburg for the summer. We'd rent a room with Miss Bessie Montgomery and Ben would travel all over the state while I played bridge and golf and tennis. We did that through 1937.

We stayed with Senator Byrnes through his second Senate race. I should say here that James Byrnes was a perfectly delightful human being. You couldn't have told to save your life where that man came from. Not from hearing him speak.

He was born and reared in Charleston but had the most beautiful diction. And he had a great gift for getting along with people and a fine sense of humor. He was a Supreme Court justice, secretary of state, director of wartime mobilization. He could have been president. He was Roosevelt's choice for vice president and it's just a fluke that the job went to Harry Truman. But most important to me, and I suppose lots of other people feel the same, Mr. Byrnes and I were really good friends. I wasn't up to drawing Mr. Byrnes out. I mean, I was from the banks of the Wassmasaw Swamp and he didn't ask me about the ways and means of the nation, but we did enjoy each other's company. He would have made a wonderful president. He had what they call the "big picture."

In 1937 Ben and I left Washington. Mr. Byrnes said, "Ben, let me assist you in getting someplace to practice law." He had clout in Spartanburg. He could have helped Ben in Washington, too. But it was a mutual decision: We did not want to live in a big city. We'd made up our minds to live in the Low Country of South Carolina and that's what we did. Ben was made an assistant district attorney based in Charleston. He made about five thousand a year, but he was also a partner in a firm. Pickings were damn slim. Ben kept at it and gradually built a very good practice. He was counsel for the county council. They met every Tuesday night. And he represented the Citadel. Ben had graduated from the Citadel. He was a good-looking man. He loved being with people. Being with all kinds.

Ben joined the Elks. We went everywhere with the Elks. Myrtle Beach. New York. That was a partying bunch of guys. And we'd dance. I fell into a tub of butter when it came to dancing. Dancing every Saturday night. Then Ben became president of the South Carolina Society. And president of the St. Andrew Society. And president of the Agriculture Society. And president of the Historic Charleston Foundation.

I am the daughter-in-law of a Confederate veteran. Ben's father fought in the Civil War. The Whaley family is from Edisto Island and the story goes that Ben's grandfather had gone off to war and was shot in the knee. It was time for his oldest boy to do his duty and go next, but that boy said, "War? No thank you. The only thing I'm interested in is liquor and women." So the honor of going to war went to Ben's father, who was only sixteen. He didn't have Ben until he was sixty-nine. The Civil War wasn't one of the great concerns of our lives, though. It certainly hadn't been for my parents. They were too busy looking forward to worry over what might have been. That war was such a waste. After the war, many of the talented and ambitious young people left the South and those who remained suffered great hardships. Still, I'll say this, those hardships brought families together. Made them loyal and helpful to each other through the tenth or eleventh cousin.

But back to Ben and me. It came as a shock at first—living in Charleston. The kind of village life I was used to, even the life we'd lived in Washington, D.C., hadn't prepared me for life here. I came from the banks of the Wassmasaw Swamp. Ben and I felt like outsiders. It definitely mattered who you were. Who your family was. It mattered who introduced you into society. It mattered that you lived below Broad Street.

And then there was the matter of where we were to go to church. The nuances of this decision were a surprise to me. In Pinopolis there was one Episcopal church, which saw a regular attendance of about twenty-five. Nan had played the organ, helped the voices in the choir stay within striking distance of each other, and supplied the altar with flowers from her own garden for most of the fifty-two Sundays in the year. Very few surprises could be rustled up under those circumstances.

When I boarded at Ashley Hall, my aunt and uncle picked me up on Sunday mornings and took me to St. Michael's Episcopal Church. It never entered my head that there would be an alternative to St. Michael's. Ben said, "What? St. Michael's? We're not going to St. Michael's." I said, "Not going to St. Michael's? What are you talking about?" St. Luke's was what he was talking about.

Not on your life, I told Ben. I'd been to St. Michael's for four years while at Ashley Hall and I didn't mean to change. He'd not been to any church in Charleston. What had got into him? "Well," he said hesitantly, "I've been thinking of going

into politics, and if we go to St. Michael's no one above Broad
Street will vote for me."

Well, I thought, if what he was saying was the absolute and
positive truth, we'd have to make a compromise. We settled
on St. Philip's, an Episcopal church within sight of our house
and above Broad Street.

People may suspect that I am an intentional eccentric—
highly and enjoyably motivated, enthusiastic, opinionated on
any and every subject. Sometimes embarrassing even to myself when I belatedly find that my homework has not been
broad or deep enough. I'd say I am probably only a modicum
different from others, though, the odd product of two different cultures. The first twenty-three years of my life were spent
in a Low Country pineland village surrounded by plantations
and plantation families. The rest of my life has been spent
being married and living in a city, a city on a peninsula,
Charleston, South Carolina, surrounded by people with very
different, much more sophisticated and worldly experiences,
and all of them with huge families—the Legares, the Hugers,
the Rutledges, the Pinckneys, the Prioleaus, the Ravenels,
Jerveys, Mazycks, Barnwells, Grimballs, Porchers, Stoneys,
Pringles, etc., etc., etc. The top count I ever heard of was one

of these gentlemen having seventeen children by one lady. All of these families intermarried and any and every dinner-party conversation was redolent with references to Cousin Harriet, Uncle Herbert, Aunt Lou, Uncle Ashmead, Aunt Charlotte. This was wholly unfathomable, simply opaque to a bride who was one of two, whose mother was one of three. I felt like writing home:

> *Dear Mrs. Fishburne,*
>
> *I'm not up to this. I'm sorry to report to you that I'm not going to make it. I'm about to drown in this tangle of relationships. There are too many people here in too close quarters.*
>
>

Your loving daughter,
Emily

I missed the privacy of the open spaces. I missed the comfortable feeling of belonging. I missed having supportive, loving family close around——family to give me direction, to point out the signposts. I missed the characters who had been onstage with me for all those early years: Cousin Bessie, who was the postmistress, Miss Mae, the telephone operator who could tell by looking out her window whether Dad was in his office or down at the train station. Now the stage was filled with a new cast of characters, all of whom seemed more or less inscrutable. I was awed by managing dowagers who enjoyed queening it over the Status Quo. Feeling very unsure of my own charms, I backed off to take a breather and to find by own direction. Finally I took sanctuary in my garden. It became my first absorbing hobby. It has been a joy and a creative adventure for more than fifty years.

I remember what Aunt Em said about a garden being a sanctuary. And how a garden should push back the wilderness and be an intimate place safe from lions and elephants, whatever was out there. A safe place that kept out the haints. The noise in the city. I've just learned to stop hearing it. You avoid listening.

But back then I wanted to buy a lot at Hobcaw. This was a new real estate development located across the Cooper River bridge, northeast of Charleston. Pinopolis was on the upper end of Berkeley County. Hobcaw was on the lower end. Still very far apart, but Hobcaw *was* the country. No houses at all at the time. I could have had a horse and a garden. I wanted to live there. But Ben, who also had grown up in the country, wanted to be in the city. The girls said that I sat in the bathtub with the door open weeping and crying very loudly about

Hobcaw so Ben Scott could hear. We finally bought a lot there, but there was no moving. That was the end of it. We actually had two lots at Hobcaw, but we eventually sold them when the children were in college and we used the money to pay bills.

I know how this sounds to you women of the nineties. Well, life doesn't always go exactly as we want, but I had other beaus. I could very easily have married someone else and stayed on in Pinopolis my entire life. But I thank my lucky stars that Ben Scott turned up. We had a happy life together in Charleston.

I don't think there's a magic answer to marriage, but maybe young people today should realize that arguments don't work. They should stop. Just stop. Nobody should speak for a few minutes and then you say, "Now listen. How can we resolve this? We're buddies. I don't win. You don't win." Often couples don't really talk things out because both are afraid of what will happen. They think a calm discussion will make things worse.

Sometimes, of course, you need to get some perspective on things before you can do a good job of talking. And that's not always so easy to do. I know that not everyone believes in using psychologists, but I do and I have found them very useful in my life. I have an excellent one and I think if you'll put your ear to the ground you can find someone just as good. When I get so involved with something I'm faced with and can't see the woods for the trees, I pay a visit to Kay, who listens intently to my tale of woe. She asks a question or two, thinks the situation over while I don't dream of interrupting, and finally says, I'd do this—one, two, and three. When I think over what she's suggested, I realize it's pure horse sense and wonder why I didn't see the light myself. Before I leave, she sees, through a bit more conversation, that I have my sense of humor back.

Every church should have one of these good psychologists on their staffs. That would doubtless cut down on divorces in their congregations. When Ben and I were married, I don't remember being counseled by the Church beforehand, and if I was I didn't listen. But the Church should be able to make three simple points. You two who are about to be married— you are teammates. You have to back each other up. And if you are not planning to do that, then don't get married.

$\mathcal{S}ocial\ \mathcal{L}ife$

MY PARENTS MET AT THE ST. CECILIA BALL. I FORGET WHY IT STARTED— the St. Cecilia Society. It might have been a choral group that turned to giving dinner dances. Anyway, all that was back in the 1700s. Membership in the St. Cecilia passes from father to son and that's the only way in. The rule is there to keep the membership from getting too big. Still, it was a huge ball this year. My daughters can't get in because they didn't marry in. But the girls who aren't in the St. Cecilia now have their own ball called the Assembly and they put on a beautiful party. Emily, my granddaughter, made her debut at the Assembly. They're all there in their white gowns. They have a cocktail party first. Scotch. Bourbon. Wine. You walk around and enjoy it and each other. The debutantes are in a receiving line. The dancing continues. The dinner tables are round. The supper is delicious. It's not overcrowded. The Assembly is lovely.

There's another party story, about a party I went to years and years ago. My Aunt Em had gone with her aunt and uncle, the Coxes, to Egypt. The Coxes were assisting in the financing of archaeological diggings over there for a Philadelphia museum, so when they visited they got the red-carpet treatment. They went two or three times and knew the people—the archaeologists, everyone. This must have been about the time they were excavating King Tut's tomb. If Em were alive she'd be 106 and she was only 19 or 20 on this trip. Anyway, the English governor fell in love with her and wanted to marry her. She didn't accept the proposal, but they remained friends. Stayed in touch. The governor eventually married a woman who already had a son and many years later Aunt Em got a letter from the governor asking her to entertain his wife and stepson when they came to Charleston. And Aunt Em, as she often did, got me to fill in for her.

Well, I never met the governor's wife, but the young man wasn't very prepossessing or attractive. I had him for the day. Nine in the morning and he said, "I'd like to see your uncle's new cottage on the Isle of Palms." This meant a drive north of town, but I was proud of the bridge and how it humped up like a camel across the harbor. I loved driving it and thought it was natural that he would want to see everything. We saw the cottage and took a walk on the beach. I also showed him Fort Moultrie at the mouth of the harbor. Coming back over the bridge I pointed out the navy yard and he said he'd like to see it. I said I'd love to show it to him. It's in Berkeley County. My part of the woods. So I showed him everything at the navy yard that was accessible. After that I showed him the rest of Charleston. By then it was five and we were both invited by the novelist Josephine Pinckney for dinner. I dropped him off at the hotel and he said he would meet me at her house and not to come by for him.

I went home and changed clothes. I got Ben Scott and went over to Jo Pinckney's a little bit late. She was introducing the stepson to everyone as they were coming in. As Ben and I came through the door, the stepson of the English governor said to me, "I'm so glad to meet you." And I said, "What? You don't know me? I've showed you around since nine o'clock this morning." My voice carries even if I whisper. Everybody in the room was simply delighted that I'd been put down. The Edmundses and the Simonses. Sam Stoney. All the movers and shakers. Oh, they teased me so. Teased me about not having enough charm to make an impression on the governor's stepson.

I was so put out, but the next day this young man was invited to see Cypress Gardens. The owner paddled him herself. She was a good-looking woman and she knew it. She was paddling him through that black shiny water and explaining to him what had been done in the garden. She noticed his head was sinking and in no time at all he was asleep right under her nose. She was incensed. She rowed to an island and motioned for a boatman to come and get her. They left him on the island in the bateau sleeping. I didn't feel so bad about myself after that, but do you know who it turned out he was? Years later we discovered that the English governor's stepson was Guy Burgess, the famous spy for the Russians. God knows what he expected to learn from me, but I did show him the navy yard and the bridge and the islands and all the harbor defenses.

There's a good bit of bridge playing in my crowd. While we may not seem to follow in our mothers' footsteps, we often do incorporate into our own lives what we have observed our mothers enjoy. For myself, this is especially true of the game of bridge. Nan enjoyed playing bridge over a very long period of time—from 1910, when she married and moved to Pinopolis, until 1979, when she was still playing once a week. By then Nan was ninety-two, and the weekly game ended only because one member of the group (who, at ninety-seven, was Nan's elder) moved to Charleston to be closer to her daughter. It would be fun to know how many friends Nan made following this pursuit. It would also be fun to know how her record of wins and losses stacked up. She played for tiny stakes, but however small, stakes somehow kept the game honest, free of any wild overbidding.

When my sister and I were nine and eleven, respectively, Nan taught us auction bridge, and as the rules changed and the game became more sophisticated and was called contract bridge she insisted that we keep up with the changes. I played a credible game by age twelve, when I was shipped off to be the youngest boarding student at Ashley Hall.

Every July of my childhood, we left the heat, mosquitoes, and ennui of the Low Country to spend two months in Flat Rock, deep in the mountains of North Carolina. Nan's first cousin and best friend, Aunt Laura Manning, and her husband, Wyndham, always spent two weeks with us. I loved to be with them. Their grown-up conversation of politics, crops, and old times was alluring. They also instigated a lot of poetry reciting. One of them would start a poem. The other would chime in with a few lines. The first would carry on, and so forth. Everyone took naps after lunch. The afternoons were for driving around the beautiful countryside. As Nan used to say, we came to know a thirty-mile-square area like the floor of our bedrooms.

The mornings, though, were for playing bridge. Aunt Laura and Nan played as a team against my sister and me. Aunt Laura hardly had time to take off her traveling hat before Nan had her seated across the card table from her. The cards, all shuffled and waiting, would be dealt and we would be off and running on an adventure in competition that provided a means by which two different generations met on an intimate basis and on a level playing field.

In Flat Rock, just across the lake from us, there was another commodious summerhouse that belonged to a big Charleston family and that was used very much the way our house was. Every bedroom was full of family, close and extended, adults and children, everyone benefiting from the taste of fresh, cool mountain air and a change of pace, solidifying family relationships. On the front piazza of that house, overlooking the lake, was a bridge table, as much a fixture as the front steps. Starting right after breakfast and ending at bedtime, a bridge game with a foursome of elders was in daily progress. It wasn't until

I was very recently playing bridge with a son of that family, a man my own age, that I understood how it was they could keep the game going perpetually the way they seemed to. He told me he was taught the game at a very young age. And though the grown-ups were the ones in the daily game on the porch, every so often one of them would have to stop for a short nap. When that happened, someone would go to the end of the piazza and call down the length of the lake to where he was usually swimming and hunting for snapping turtles— cooters. Thebe! Thebe! Get on in here—we need you for a while. He and several other of those children made themselves very useful and learned to play good bridge in a pinch!

There's another tradition in Charleston I should mention here. It's been in vogue for a couple of centuries. As old as the St. Cecilia probably. It's Charlestonians giving black-tie dinner parties in their gardens during the last week in April and the first week of May. The Confederate jasmine and magnolias are in bloom, the moon is often full, and the mockingbirds sing at night. There was one such evening more than forty years ago that will always be with me. It was at the Pink House on Rainbow Row. A party of about thirty, all dressed in their festive best, all delighted to be included and knowing they were in for a memorable evening. Our hostess was sophisticated, sensitive, experienced, and an artist when it came to such evenings. Her husband was a charming accomplice. Forty years and I still look back on that evening as a gift from the two of them.

Such a house. Mellow and beautifully cared for antiques and Oriental rugs everywhere. Butlers were serving the drinks. Seasoned professionals, men who took pride in their performance. They knew what you would drink and served it with impeccable courtesy. Maids threaded their way among the guests with tasty, hot hors d'oeuvres.

When we arrived the moon was just rising over the harbor and an hour later, as we went down to dinner in the garden, it had just cleared the rooftops and was flooding every corner with silvery light. The scene we came upon could have been taken from a hardly believable romantic dream. All of our senses were assailed at once. The fragrance of the tiny ivory-colored blossoms of the Confederate jasmine, which is almost but not quite as heady as that of the gardenia, was a never-to-be-forgotten part of the evening. Flowering vines climbed up along the winding wrought-iron stairway to the long balcony above. A light breeze was stirring the white blossoms on the oleanders and was just enough to flutter the candlelight. On the low wall that separated the garden into two parts were candleholders made from handsome balustrades borrowed from some long-forgotten piazza. The light sea breeze picked up the pale blue-gray smoke rising from the candles and wafted it upward into the deep blue moonlit sky. The moon seemed to be ours alone.

We fell silent as we gazed at this opulent scene. A moment in time. Never to be repeated. When we became aware again of our companions, the voices of intimate friends began to float up and over the garden as everyone looked for their dinner seats. Small marble-topped tables, each lit by shaded candles, had been placed around the perimeter of the garden, keeping all voices from intruding on the overall ambience. The evening flowed serenely and delightfully on. Seafood of several kinds, rice, fresh asparagus, delicious homemade breads, and the host's favorite dessert—all accompanied by well-chosen chilled wine. The moon slipped behind a magnolia tree where, on the topmost branch, silhouetted against the sky, a mockingbird sat serenading the night.

It was a perfect evening. Without the lovely garden and the sensitivity and skills of our hosts, the evening would have been a happy and pleasing occasion, but not one that would have been remembered after forty years.

Preservation

~~~❦~~~

HEN BEN AND I CAME TO
CHARLESTON IN 1937 WE RENTED
128 Church Street. A year later we bought
our home at 58 Church Street. The Historic Charleston Foundation was not yet in full force. Ideas of preserving the city
were in the backs of the minds of Albert Simons, Harriet
Smythe, Josephine Pinckney, and a lot of others. Frances
Smythe Edmunds had been brought up in a house where this
discussion was going on. All her parents' friends had talked
about it—how to stop the destruction of these priceless old
houses. Frances came from a family that was confident about
dealing with anything, so she didn't hesitate when she was
asked to be the executive director of a new preservation organization. The old preservationists were beginning to die off,
but Frances was young and had her dander up. She would take
on anybody. Charleston wouldn't begin to look the way it
does today if it hadn't been for her willingness to make ene-

mies anywhere. Practically speaking, she saved the city and put it back on the map.

Ben Scott was the second president of Historic Charleston. Frances, as I've said, was the executive director. She'd come up with the ideas. Ben had the lawyerly skills, plus you could call him at midnight. In fact, he made himself officially available to Historic Charleston for telephone consultation at each and every midday, if need be. He helped do the bylaws and was president for thirteen years. I can't say she used him as a sounding board, but when it came to broadening the base of Historic Charleston, she did listen to him. They brought in businessmen and others. At first it was just a little downtown group—just a board with no members—but Ben helped to expand the group. They asked people to open their houses for tours and they charged money for these tours. They bought and saved 51 Meeting Street. It was for sale, and with its big garden it might very well have been cut into lots. Mr. Smith Richardson said, "I will give Historic Charleston $35,000 if you can match it." The board went to everybody for that matching money. Children gave dimes and nickles through schools and the property was bought. That was in the late 1940s. Frances Edmunds did that and Mrs. Elizabeth Jenkins

Young from Edisto did the same kind of thing, saving the houses around the College of Charleston. But you can't really say it was all done by one person or even two. It was also Nancy Stevenson, who had the vision to put all the garden tours on during one month. In April glorious garden tours are held on Wednesday afternoons. They are a sellout. The profits go into a revolving fund that makes it possible to buy threatened houses. And Patti Whitelaw has been a constant source of know-how and help of all kinds. Many other people are deeply involved as well. Many. But the success of Historic Charleston shows that one strong-willed person can move mountains.

Of course, there is a downside. Back in the thirties, when all this was just beginning to be discussed, I don't think anyone could have imagined the impact that the resulting tourism would have. The carriage rides, the traffic, thousands of people coming to Charleston instead of going to Europe.

Of course, it's flattering in a way, having such enthusiastic visitors. And there have been other benefits that are often overlooked. Years ago the only two places to go to dinner were the yacht club and Henry's. The restaurant food in Charleston was extremely poor. Now you have a half dozen top restaurants.

And I think the longtime residents appreciate what's here more than they once did. They understand the architecture. It's not just the appearance that's been spruced up. Now you can attend eight lectures each year given by people who know what they're talking about. You can learn about periods of furniture and about silversmiths and furniture makers or how to recognize the period of a house by glancing at the roof. All this has brought the beauty of Charleston home to the old inhabitants. We do enjoy it more with this depth of knowledge.

Still, some of the big houses are being cut up into condominiums and the taxes have gone up and up. That taxes have gone up is not really the fault of tourism, though.

The one thing I can't stand—what I absolutely know is bad news—is when you see people in costumes. It's a stage set then. Those Confederate uniforms you see on the carriage drivers. The carriages themselves have hurt us. They make the city a stage set. At first there was just one carriage, with a driver named Harry. Harry and his horses were a part of Charleston. His black-and-white fox terrier sat beside him on the seat. He gave children rides. He'd driven carriages in Vienna and his horses were fresh and beautifully kept. The harnesses were top-drawer. We were proud of him. These carriages today are just an absolute nuisance. You encounter three or four just getting to the grocery store. I have a friend who's a watercolorist. She heard one coming once and threw a basin of her brush water onto the driver. But that's not a long-term solution.

Even so, the tourist business is still a plus for the city. I think we have a very forward-looking mayor in Joe Riley. He's done a wonderful job. Most of us mind very much the aquarium that's planned. You can see aquariums in other cities and every year the proposed price goes up and up. Nobody is excited about paying higher taxes, but I like Mayor Riley. He sees ahead and has the clout to carry everybody in Charleston on his back. That hasn't made everyone happy. It's made some furious, but he has the vision and the clout and Charleston is a perfectly delightful place to live in and to come to. Great hotels. Delicious food. Something to do every minute. Gardens to visit. Houses to tour. I don't know of another city where six days a week five beautiful houses are open to visitors. The Nathaniel Russell with its flying staircase. The Edmondston-Alston, which looks out over the harbor. The Manigault and Heyward-Washington houses with their wonderful furniture. The Aiken-Rhett House with its two rooms that remained locked up for more than seventy years. You have all this and just outside the city are Magnolia and Middleton gardens. Visitors can get the true flavor of the city. They can go through these houses and gardens and see how people used to live, can sense the leisure and warmth and wealth that went into the city's character. More to the point, residents of the city have an opportunity to share what they love.

I've mentioned this before. My lecture on civic pride, which I came by honestly being Nan's daughter. Nan and her gardener went to Moncks Corner and planted two public flower beds. She put one by the train station and a second one by the bank. She not only planted them but she maintained them afterwards. If you're proud of your village or your city, you're happy to share it.

My garden would not begin to be the fun and satisfaction that it is for me if I didn't open it for charitable causes. There were eighteen formal tours of my garden this April with all the proceeds going to charity. People come to Charleston from every part of the U.S.A. March, April, May, and June —if a visitor is garden oriented there's a good chance he or she will see my garden. Both Nan and my Aunt Em convinced me of this. Aunt Em opened her own garden and told me firmly that if you have something beautiful you should share it. Gardens above all else are for sharing. Growing up in Pinopolis taught me that as well. And there is a dividend. I feel my garden has brought pleasure to others and possibly inspired them. And visitors sometimes put pen to paper to tell me so. You may be sure that this brings pleasure back to me. I like it! Yes!

Cooking

I ALSO LIKE PEOPLE TO BREAK BREAD WITH ME, BUT EXPERT HELP IN THE kitchen is expensive. I really love to have people by two or three times a week. It's an adventure being with people on a one-on-one basis. I need to offer bait and my cooking is my bait. Dinner, lunch, or just a sugar cookie. If I can put forth a good product I can lure them. People are the greatest—the most fun that life offers and you can enjoy them sitting down. No mountain climbing. No hair-raising sailing before the mast. You don't have to be muscled up and twenty years old to take part in this kind of adventure.

No, it's not such a struggle. I am not the least bit shy with any kind of person. You get over being shy if you're really interested in what you're hearing and seeing. How does his or her mind work? What are their politics? Their religion? I am interested. Even now at this age I'm hoping to learn and hoping to be entertained. I'm delving.

But to get back to entertaining—that is, cooking for people. I adore recipes. But I hardly ever try anything that doesn't have a picture. Or that I haven't eaten at somebody's house. People will give you the recipe if you ask. Like gardening, cooking is something people want to share with others. And then I've got the recipe and I use it to bring people to my house. This was good for Ben, too. He was always making friends and nothing makes friends faster than having people to your house on a casual basis. When they're comfortable and you're comfortable and they know that you've taken some trouble. I try to teach my grandchildren that they don't need to serve steaks. Steak might be the absolutely most delicious thing on earth, but a person you are trying to make a friend of may not have the money to keep up with you. Keep it simple. Don't spend big money. Just make it delicious and serve it casually. Let them know you want to give them a treat, but really and truly you're treating yourself to their personality.

It has always surprised me so. I used to think I was reaching out over my head here—that these people didn't want to come to my house. But an invitation to a person is the biggest compliment you can pay them. And you do want it to go smoothly. Before my company comes I have things ready to move. I'm confident. I've expended plenty of elbow grease before the door opens. Take trouble and time. It pays off in confidence. If you're confident, then you're relaxed.

As for seating arrangements—you definitely don't want husbands and wives sitting together. If that goes on then the purpose of the party has been ruined. A party is for an exchange. I used to tell Ben Scott, "This is perfectly ridiculous. I've got nothing to tell you when I get back from the party if I'm by your side and you've got not one damn thing to tell me. We're not having this. No! You're not to sit by your wife." And I've learned another thing. Never invite best friends to come to your house in a small gathering. They talk to each other. Forget it. If I can manage it, I tell two or three of my guests, "You are seated by such and such, so don't spend time with that person before dinner." I want them to come to the table fresh for conversation.

Seating the young and the old? Again that shouldn't matter. Conversation is a skill. There was the wife of a columnist here. An older woman. A woman of experience, I should say. I was thirtyish. She had a gift. She would sit me down by her and say, "What are you up to?" She could draw you out. It was her hobby, I suppose. Drawing people out. Making them feel like she was talking to the most important person on earth. Not a bad pastime. Far better than most.

So that's it for the art of entertaining and conversation. I should repeat that Nan made us practice. Her dinnertime efforts were frustrating, I'm sure—but still, entertaining might be like gardening. Something in the blood. An entertaining gene. The people in our family were (and are) very gregarious. They like getting together. Even 150 years ago you hear of them dancing. Singing. Playing the guitar. On both sides— my mother and father came from people with gregarious genes. Full of life and—very luckily—healthy, strong people. They lived to old ages. Nan lived to ninety-four and Dad was eighty-seven. Mother's sister and two first cousins all lived to be ninety-seven.

It's an awful lot of fun to live into your eighties. It helps to have some money, though. Let's get that right. The bottom line is, you have to have some money if you don't want to be dependent on other people. And I'm grateful. You bet your sweet life I'm grateful, and I hope I use it right. I've worked but I've worked at things I enjoy. Being married to Ben meant a lot of entertaining. I hate to call it entertaining because it wasn't grand. But we always had an open house—a welcoming house—and that required elbow grease. My elbow grease. And I was proud and grateful that I could do it. My parents' house was the same. In Pinopolis there would even be people to breakfast. I remember Cousin Isaac Porcher on a hot summer day eating fried red breast bream at the table. Hominy. Waffles. Lord knows why Dad wasn't square.

Nan made blackberry wine in demijohns. She'd tell Catherine, the cook, to spread the word on Sunday at church. Anybody who'd like to bring in blackberries, she'd buy any amount. They'd start coming in. Nan and Catherine would have all these demijohns of blackberry wine they were working on. My daughter Anne has found that recipe book and has made several gallons of blackberry wine. The last time I tasted blackberry wine was a long time ago. I don't think I appreciated it then as I would today. I'd like to know how much strength it had to it. And Nan always bought pound cake. Anybody who came to see Nan, they'd sit down. Maybe on the joggling board or on the side piazza. Maybe in her dining room. Wherever. They'd have a glass of blackberry wine and a piece of pound cake. And another thing she always had was "thin sweet cake." This was little squares of, yes, thin sweet cake.

The recipes for all this are in the cookbook Anne found. The University of South Carolina Press gave her three readers for the manuscript and one of them happened to be a cookbook author who owns a restaurant in Charleston. He's a well-known chef and has written fascinating cookbooks. He looked over Anne's book and said he knew all of these recipes. He'd put a lot of them in one of his own books. What had happened was Nan had her garden club, which was originally the Civic League. I told you how Nan and everybody else had absolutely no money. Well, there was a black man called Henry Thomson who had a one-horse wagon and a mule and worked for hire. The village had areas that belonged to nobody. Places that would grow up in thickets unless somebody

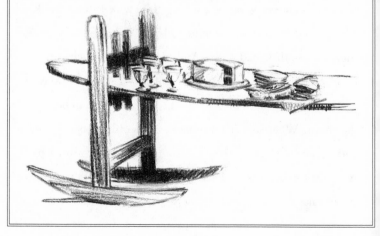

grubbed them. Nan wasn't the kind to cut off anything. The roots must be removed as well. Nan said to the Civic League, "Let's get our recipes together. I have this old recipe book of my mother's and you all have recipes from the plantations— North Hampton, Summerton, everywhere. Let's collect these things together." So they did and somebody typed out numerous copies. They were put into loose-leaf notebooks. Pretty covers of cloth were made and the Civic League sold them and used the money to pay Henry Thomson.

Well, one of Nan's sisters lived in Boston and was always interested in helping Nan with one of the forty projects she always had going right up til the week she died. The sister in Boston helped sell those books around to make money for Henry Thomson's grubbing. I can see Henry right now. He had a pickax. When I visited, Nan would say, "Come with me. I want to see how Henry is doing." But I'm drifting from the subject, which is my prerogative at eighty-five, I should add.

One day this famous cookbook writer was walking down the sidewalk in Boston and he saw some boxes set out. Boxes where someone had moved or was cleaning house and that had been put out for the trash man. And there, sticking out of this debris, was the Pinopolis cookbook. He took it home and tried the recipes. He liked them and included them in his own cookbook, which proves that it's a small world. Or that you can't keep a good recipe down.

I've included a few very simple recipes of my own in this chapter, ones that I've borrowed from high and low and ones that I'm happy to pass along. Serve them in your garden. Use them as your snare. You don't have to follow them exactly. I just tend to stand around the stove and put in ingredients til it suits me. The dump method—sprinkle and taste, sprinkle and taste.

My forebears were all interested in good food. Nan and my Aunt Em had been all over Europe and seen all the flower gardens. They could design a garden as well as anybody at that time. Aunt Em's garden was filled with statues and laid out with focal points. The most beautiful flowers. But the first thing Aunt Em would say when she got off the train in Moncks Corner was, "Nan, did you get up a stand of spinach?" That generation, as I've told you, they had grown up in places where the store did not provide spinach, lettuce, or any of the other amenities for a table. The honey came from local bees. Everything that went on their tables, with the exception of rice, flour, salt, sugar, and cans of salmon—there were cases of canned salmon in every house—came from the vegetable garden. Aunt Em's favorite was a hot bed with mushrooms. My grandmother had specialized in asparagus, which she'd brought along from her Virginia beginnings. So if you have the space, a vegetable garden is a wonderful shortcut to the table. But if you don't have the space and have chosen flowers and shrubs over vegetables, nowadays you at least have the delight of browsing the supermarket's produce.

I should also mention that I've deer hunted and been on deer drives, but I wouldn't shoot a deer for anything in the world. I've turned against hunting. It's an anachronism. In the first place, you may get a duck, but how many times has it flown the flyways? It's likely to be tough no matter what you do to it. A wild turkey is the most awful meal to serve a guest. Think of the kind of muscles it has! Better to go to the super-market. Dad's generation was the last to supply their own table. There was a reason back then, but now every bit of wildlife is going down the drain. Duck hunting. It's a reason to get out of your bed and you do see the sunrise. The dew and the first light on the marsh. A flying duck sounds like nothing else. But I won't shoot. How awful. How useless. Of course, you don't talk that way around men or teach your daughters to talk that way around men, but bird-watchers have the right idea. Bird-watching is a wonderful turn of events.

Someone stopped me on the street the other day and said, "I want to bring you some partridges." I said, "No, thank you." She said, "They're all cleaned." I still said, "No, thank you." I said, "I don't like ducks, either." "How about venison?" I said, "Absolutely not." I said, "The only thing you can bring me is Tyson chicken breast. I want it bought out of a store and I want it tender."

One of my favorite recipes for chicken breasts is also one of the simplest. First, make a marinade using ⅓ cup Dijon mustard, ¼ cup white wine, and 3 teaspoons honey. Stir the marinade thoroughly and place 6 skinless, boneless chicken breasts in it for 1 hour. While the breasts are marinating, preheat the oven to 500°F and make the breading mixture. This mixture requires 2 cups fine bread crumbs and 1 cup grated extra-sharp cheddar cheese. After the chicken has marinated, roll it in the breading mixture and place it in a greased baking pan, uncovered. Sprinkle some extra breading mixture over the top of the chicken and then bake the chicken for 10 to 12 minutes in the preheated oven. If you're not going to serve the chicken immediately, cut off the oven and leave the door slightly cracked. But don't let it sit in the oven for too long!

I got this next recipe from a woman in the shank of life. The shank of life. That's young. Young enough, anyway. Fifty maybe. I never want to go back to my twenties, my teens, or thirties. From forty-five on is when life begins, so this is a recipe with some authority behind it. I should add that the shrimp man was still coming up Church Street in the 1960s. Some streets in Charleston still have a shrimp man. It used to be that a tin plate piled up high was twenty-five cents. Piled up with fresh shrimp, I mean, and he had a call—a song he sang. There are still a few vendors working the other streets. They bring crab and shrimp. A city like Charleston, on the coast, well, seafood is a natural, but this shrimp dish is a soufflé, so you can't serve it in the garden.

You have to prepare this shrimp casserole the day before you plan to serve it. You will need:

> *6 to 8 slices white bread, crusts*
> *removed and torn into pieces*
>
> *2 pounds fresh shrimp, cooked and shelled*
>
> *½ pound Old English cheddar cheese,*
> *sliced and torn into pieces*

½ cup unsalted butter, melted

1 teaspoon dry mustard

½ teaspoon mace

1 teaspoon salt

1 teaspoon Worcestershire sauce

2 cups half-and-half cream

3 eggs, lightly beaten

Place a layer of torn bread pieces in a greased casserole dish. Cover with a layer of shrimp and then one of cheese. Repeat the layers of bread and shrimp and cheese and then top with one more layer of torn bread pieces. Pour the melted butter evenly over the top layer of bread. Then mix together the seasonings, Worcestershire sauce, half-and-half, and lightly beaten eggs. I do this in a blender. Pour this mixture over the layers, making sure it reaches to the top layer of bread. Cover and place in the refrigerator overnight. The next day, remove the casserole from the refrigerator an hour before baking and allow to come to room temperature. Preheat the oven to 350°F. Bake the shrimp casserole, covered, for an hour in the preheated oven and serve immediately. You'll find that this dish is excellent bait for guests.

Junior Robinson gave me the following recipe. It's how his wife makes conch soup and Junior says it keeps him feeling young. His wife said, "I like to cook it a long time and cut up the conch small so the young ones can eat it too." She takes 5 to 15 live conches, large and small, and drops them into a big pot of boiling salted water, shells and all, for 30 minutes. She then removes them from the boiling water and spreads them out on wire racks to cool. When they are cool, she cuts the meat out of the shells and cuts it into small pieces. She puts the meat into a pot and just covers it with water and adds some diced onion, salt and Accent, all to taste. The soup simmers for 4 or 5 hours, until the meat is tender. But remember: Big conches are tougher than small ones and take considerably longer to reach tender stage.

We were once in one of those Low Country hurricanes and my son-in-law Fred said, "Do you have the makings of a lemon pie?" We'd been in the house with the shutters shut, humid, and all this banging—everything banging. Oh, it was hot and they were trying to entertain themselves and Fred says, "Do you have the makings of a lemon pie?" He went out to the store in the middle of this storm and bought the ingredients. The pie recipe is his grandfather's. His son Kershaw makes it too. Kershaw can go in the kitchen and make up the most luscious recipes. He's eighteen.

For the crust of Fred's lemon pie, mix together 15 crushed vanilla wafers, ¼ cup softened unsalted butter, and ½ cup sugar. Press this mixture into the *bottom* of a pie dish and place whole vanilla wafers around the *sides* of the dish. For the filling, blend together 3 egg yolks (save the egg whites) and ½ cup lemon juice. Slowly add 1 can condensed milk. Pour the filling into the crust and bake the pie in a preheated 375°F oven for 7 minutes. Remove the pie from the oven and let it cool.

Of course, no lemon pie is complete without a meringue. Whip the 3 egg whites with ½ teaspoon cream of tartar. Add ½ cup sugar, 1 tablespoon at a time. Add a pinch of salt. Spoon the meringue over the pie in pretty peaks, then set the pie under the broiler with the door open because you have to watch it every minute. As soon as the meringue turns light tan, take the pie out of the oven and refrigerate it for 2 hours or so before serving.

This last recipe is one from Pinopolis, Nan's thin sweet cake I mentioned, though I've added a few convenient modern touches to her "company" cake.

Preheat the oven to 375°F. Using a food processor, which Nan did not have the luck to have, combine 2 cups sifted all-purpose flour, ⅛ teaspoon salt, 1 cup sugar, 1 egg, and 9 table-spoons softened unsalted butter. Twirl these ingredients until they all come together as a ball. Press the mixture evenly into a 16" × 10" baking pan that has been well buttered. Sprinkle with sugar and cinnamon and bake in the preheated oven for 10 to 12 minutes. Remove the cake from the oven and let it cool slightly. Meanwhile, reduce the oven temperature to 200°F. Cut the cake into tea-size squares, place on wire racks, and return to the oven for 1 hour. This will dry out and crisp up the squares.

> *From rich chocolate mousse*
> *To boiled okra and rice,*
> *Just settle in now*
> *And savor each bite.*

Rosie

OSIE, THE END OF THIS MEMOIR IS APPROACHING AND I'VE TOLD YOU practically nothing about my dog, Rosie. She's a Jack Russell terrier whose age, like most ladies' ages, is a tightly held secret. Why don't we say that's she's five years old and holding—an age that I've chosen because most dogs have to reach about five to become sophisticated and self-directed and to acquire a well-developed role in life. She and I accept the fact that her business is keeping the burglars out of the house and the cats out of the garden. Plus she's the official greeter at the front door—she makes the decisions about who is to come in and who is not welcome. And of course, most importantly, she is my companion, through thick and thin, twenty-four hours a day.

I like to read in bed at night and while I do this she happily sleeps under my bed. But as soon as I turn out the light she gets into bed. If it's warm weather, she sleeps at the extreme

foot. If at about 4:00 A.M. it begins to be a bit chilly, she snuggles in and is like a comfortable hot-water bottle.

It's my habit to drink coffee in the morning in the garden. Both of us love doing this. I might wander around checking on plants here and there or realizing that the alignments in one place or another aren't perfect. Or that maybe another area could take a lot of improvement, and I'm wondering why I hadn't seen it before. Rosie, in the meantime, is easing through a border. She's surefooted like Junior and never disturbs a single plant as she prowls. Or she might, with absolute delight, run up to a late-sleeping cat and chase it up a wall. When all that is attended to, she sits on one hip on the brick paving. She sits in the strategic middle, which allows her to see both ends of the garden, and she keeps an eye out for the slightest movement of the shrubs. Her ears are cocked, her eyes and body alert, and she is listening to sounds near and far and enjoying the breezes. Or she lies on the hot rocks in the middle of the day to treat her arthritis. I know dogs can be trouble, and yes, Rosie is sweetmeat for fleas. I can't leave her, though. Not even for a week. She wouldn't eat. I can't leave her.

Self-Esteem

SELF-ESTEEM IS ANOTHER SUBJECT THAT I SEEM TO HAVE PUT OFF UNTIL LAST. Can I talk about it in a book about gardening? You bet. What I want to say is that the amount of energy taken up hating—it's so destructive. I mean on the level of personal relationships. That kind of hatred can be so petty. So hurtful. It undermines a person's self-confidence. It doesn't allow a person to reach her potential. That's each person's God-given right—to be the best, to do the best she can—but it won't happen if others cut her down, put her in her place. There's too much competition. I don't mean the healthy kind of competition that goes into a tennis match or a bridge game or making the most beautiful garden. I mean the kind that cripples people. I'd rather compete only with myself. Make my own product better every single time. Give somebody else a boost when I get the chance. Don't put others down. Don't set out to better others just for the sake of being better. This is

what it will take to make a better world. Reach your top potential and let the chips fall where they may. I made up my
mind a long time ago to fill up my life with constructive
things. There's a space there between the ears and if it's filled
with the right ideas the destructive thoughts just can't get in.
Planting to keep the weeds out. There just isn't room for both.

To Conclude

*I*T'S BEEN WONDERFUL — PUTTING TO-
GETHER THIS MEMOIR — BUT THE POR-
tions about Pinopolis have made me homesick for
old times. Back then people were in and out of each other's
gardens. They'd be strolling and admiring, kibitzing about
soils and successes and failures of planting or just sitting and
passing the time of day. People were so closely connected.
When anyone had an important occasion — a wedding, a bap-
tism, a confirmation, or a funeral — those in charge of decorations knew without asking that everyone's flowers and
greens were available for the occasion.

As mother's garden was right next to the church, she
supplied the flowers for the church altar on most of the
Sundays of the year. Even if someone had wanted to buy a
florist's flowers for the altar it would have been almost impossible. Store-bought flowers would have had to be sent up on
the afternoon train from Charleston. It never crossed any-

one's mind to think of such a thing. And anyway, our lovely fresh flowers were far more varied and beautiful. Our church was kept exquisitely clean and polished. The lovely hand-embroidered linens were all made and done up proudly by the ladies of the church.

At Christmas there would be smilax and holly gathered from the nearby woods and at Easter we had little white naked swamp lilies and pale pink wild azaleas to dress the church. We children were allowed to gather the lilies and it was a looked-forward-to occasion. Cousin Carrie. She was the instigator of these flower and berry gatherings. It was she, you remember, she and her sister, Cousin Kitty, who made spending money by making baby bonnets and sending them to Charleston on the morning train to be sold at the Ladies Exchange on King Street. And it was Cousins Carrie and Kitty who after a time were able to save up enough money for the gentle black horse they appreciatively named Bonnet. On special occasions, Cousin Carrie would hitch up Bonnet to the buggy and we would meet her at the church and every child would squeeze in. Off she would drive, down the white sandy road to Fanny Branch, that shallow, sherry-colored stream running through the middle of a quite open swamp area that bordered the length of the village. The word *snake* was never mentioned. No one was afraid of snakes, anyhow. When we arrived at our destination, she would pull Bonnet to a halt and we would jump out.

I want you to see it. I want you to understand. We were all barefoot—barefoot was our usual state—and barefoot we would fan out through the swamp making sweeps for the little white lilies. When we had a fistful of these (loosely held, please!) flowers, we'd run back to Cousin Carrie, who had a bucket of water ready. We'd pick enough to fill every vase the church owned. Then we'd pile back in the buggy and head for the church, where the grown-ups were waiting to decorate with our lilies and the wild azaleas that had been gathered in the woods earlier that morning.

There would always be a boy or two who would be specially incorporated into the procedures. They'd climb the ladders and help clean up. This was especially so at Christmastime, when the swags of smilax had to be draped over every window. The windows were tall with ancient panes of clear glass. Through them I could watch our horses grazing under the big mature pines. Quite a lovely and sometimes distracting sight. Yes.

We grew up playing hide-and-seek in the village gardens. We hunted Easter eggs in those gardens. We climbed up on the scuppernong grape arbors in September and stuffed ourselves with the fragrant sun-warmed fruits. The bees would share these with us. We grew up in *all* the houses and gardens of the village, where everyone welcomed us and was interested in us. We learned about plants and the pleasures of gardening became a part of each one of us. Though we were married in our churches, most of us had our receptions in the gardens. In our garden there was a big spreading live oak tree that earned the name the Wedding Tree.

When I was about eleven years old—I know I was still not wearing shoes, still barefoot the year-round—Nan told me that she and I were to be on the program at the United Daughters of the Confederacy meeting at Cousin Betty Dwight's one afternoon. We were going to play our piano duets. I was to go with her but stay outside until after the business portion of the meeting. She'd call me when our time came to perform.

This all suited me fine. There was a wonderful tree in Cousin Betty's backyard. Nan went on inside and I climbed the tree, to the very top. The tree swayed gently in a light breeze. I could see over all the village.

Every age has its joys. If we could climb trees in our old age, probably every treetop would be full of elders swaying in the breeze. When Nan called, I shinnied down and ran into the meeting. Playing duets with my mother was duck soup. She took charge—I was just along for the ride. I loved tunes, rhythm, the sounds of a piano, the fun of playing with her. The sounds were so much richer in a duet, and since she played the treble I was part of a more sophisticated level of music than I could have reached by myself.

No. Nothing untoward happened. I didn't fall out of the tree. I didn't mess up my part of the duets. I'm telling this story because of the warmth that emanated toward me from that room full of the grown-up women of the village. Here were the grown-ups who helped raise us, who followed our ups and downs with such sympathy, sometimes applauding, sometimes wiping our tears away. They were just there, interested in our every move, and their larders of thin ginger cakes, homemade pickles, and fat biscuits were there for us, too. How glad I am that I am eighty-five years old and can look back with such gratitude and pleasure on their values and their care of us. I think I am more aware of them now that I've reached this hoary age than I've ever been.

I remember that afternoon, when the applause was loud and clear and the hugs plentiful and sweet, with joy that a moment like that isn't lost in time.

And before Pinopolis there was my grandmother Anne gardening at Belvidere Plantation. And before that her mother-in-law, Emily Wharton Sinkler, writing in the 1840s to her father in Philadelphia telling him how she was "scouring the countryside" for slips of roses, for starts from her neighbors that she would turn into her own fine garden. All of it was about sharing. Especially Pinopolis, whose influence I don't think I can ever escape. Back there we shared our acres, our gardens, our children, our thoughts, and our time with each other. And through this we were bound together in a community, a community of interests—some of these interests wonderful and productive and, yes, some bad. We were there with each other through thick and thin, whether or not we were of the same blood or same social background, or the same faith or the same color. We belonged to each other.

Late in his life, my husband, Ben Scott, would sit with Rosie on the bench in front of the house. So many people are traveling. Tourists. You really don't get the feel of a place unless you can get into a house or a garden. If you travel yourself you

realize this. People would be walking—walking in our climate—and I'd always wanted to put a bench outside. But Ben wouldn't let me. He said somebody would run into it and what all.

Anyway, when he got to the place where he wasn't in such good shape, I put the bench out there and he started sitting on it. If he went out there without Rosie—he would so often forget her—Rosie would go at that door. Oh, you never heard such. I'd let her out and they'd sit on the bench and he'd talk to everyone who went up and down Church Street. He'd find out where they were from and then he'd always ask what they had seen and whether they were having a good time. Then he'd say, "Would you like to see my wife's garden?" Yes, they'd love to see his wife's garden. He'd say, "Make sure to go all the way to the back." So they'd tour the garden by themselves, then come back out and have another conversation with him. And this would go on all day, morning and afternoon. People found Ben charming and they thought Rosie was the cutest thing.

Nobody actually wrote poetry amongst us, no real jinglers, but now when I get out of bed in the morning I always say:

> *Rosie,*
> *It's time to be up and doing,*
> *With a heart for any fate.*
> *Still achieving, still pursuing,*
> *Learn to labor and to wait.*

And Rosie jumps up like a shot. She knows exactly what that means. She knows it's time to move.

Ben said that poem before he got up every morning. Ben won a contest saying that at school. But I knew it, too. We had learned our poetry. "The Village Blacksmith." Those hot summer afternoons when I was caught at loose ends. I had to recite on forever.

Something else that would drive me wild as a child. Nan would say, "Don't go off too far. We're going to such and such in a few minutes." I'd be sitting down on the bottom step waiting, but what a person of my mother's age thought of as a minute was not what I thought of as a minute. That minute would drag on. I'd say, "When are you coming?" Just a minute darling. I'll be right there. Another ten minutes would pass and for me that was an eternity. I've heard others say this. Our idea of time alters as we age. You think, Why write down any of this? This is the way it's going to be for the next thousand years and then suddenly time is racing by. It's perfectly fantastic how little time I have and how full my day is.

I feel I was born under a lucky star, blessed with vigorous health, a great deal of energy, and the inheritance of two genes that are my true aces in the hole: enthusiasm and *joie de vivre*. Over all my years, despite my dismal academic record, I have become a jack-of-all-trades, dipping in and out of half a dozen interests—gardening, sewing, cooking, piano playing, writing, painting, and bridge—and coming nowhere near star quality in any of them but enjoying them all constantly. I'm surprised that I've kept being intensely interested and I'm surprised by how much expertise one does build up little by little. One thing I've figured out is that no one is going to be able to find me in the end. Why? Because I will have been swallowed up and entirely disappeared from view amongst the quantity of equipment that I have gathered around me to pursue these hobbies. A bloodhound will have to be brought in to find me. Gardening books, hoes and rakes, plants and benches and water pumps, oils and watercolors and brushes and easels, folding tables, cans of turpentine, sewing machine attachments, boxes of bobbins, patterns by the hundreds, baskets of embroidery thread, and let's not even list the cooking equipment!

Amazing. The days just fly. You cannot fit it all in. When you get to eighty-five, it's going like a bullet.

An Appendix
of Garden
Do's and Don'ts

FERTILIZER

DO · *Early to bed, Early to rise, Work like hell and fertilize.*

My neighbor, who has just lately retired from the ministry, got this advice from a close and sympathetic friend. And it's largely true—at least the part about working like hell and fertilizing.

In September, your plants may appear bedraggled and barely blooming. Cut them back and give them a shot of the following elixir: Get a couple of three-liter plastic soft-drink bottles and using a funnel add one handful of dehydrated cow manure and one handful of 10-10-10 commercial fertilizer to each. Fill each bottle with water and shake. Put them aside for three days and shake thoroughly again before giving to your geraniums, impatiens, and bedding plants. You should wet the soil pretty thoroughly. If the plants respond happily, repeat in a week, having watered with spigot water once in the interim.

MULCH

DO · mulch your entire garden with pine needles in the fall and spring, particularly under the camellias, azaleas, roses, and larger shrubs. And also cover all bare ground with needles. This keeps the earth at an even temperature, discourages weeds, and gives the garden a neat and comfortable appearance. And the pine needles are a pretty color.

GROUND COVERS

DO · use ivy, strawberry begonia, ajuga, sedum, blue phlox, and ferns as ground covers. Where these get established you will not be troubled by weeds.

WATER

DO · water your plants in the morning so that the leaves are dry by nightfall. You'll have less trouble with fungal diseases.

SLUGS

DO · get rid of slugs. If you begin to notice that an unseen and uninvited diner is making lace of the leaves of your bedding plants and azaleas, settle jar tops full of beer on the soil close by. In the morning you'll probably find them filled with drowned slugs. Empty and refill as often as needed. The slugs are attracted to the smell of beer. They drown either because they can't swim or because they're drunk. Either way, that's it for the slugs!

COLOR LEVELS

D O · raise the level of color in your borders to six or eight feet. Using hollyhocks, delphiniums, snapdragons, foxglove, and larkspur should do it. The pointed shape of these plants will complement the round-faced flowers below them—not only in the garden but in flower arrangements as well. Flowering vines and hanging baskets also bring the color up. Lavender, lantana, and perennial verbena are good choices for trouble-free baskets.

For all the bedding plants, use about seven to nine of a variety in each group depending on the space available and the size of the plants. Put at least three plants together in the center of the group, one on each side of these three, and two on each end, being sure to intermingle them with the plants from the adjacent grouping. Avoid creating those squares of color that give such an awkward appearance to a border.

PINCHING

D O · pinch the tops out of flowers. This makes them put out branches and keeps them from looking leggy. Last spring we pulled up chairs and picked about three inches off the tops off all Miss Em's chrysanthemums. We then pulled the leaves off the bottoms—that's not really pinching, though. We pinched them after they rooted. Doing it yourself prevents that uniform store-bought look. You'll notice that the chrysanthemums you buy have been pinched too carefully so that you end up with a mass of color but no sense of the shape of the individual flowers. But remember: Don't pinch after July 1.

ROOTING BUCKETS
AND OTHER ROOTING TIPS

DO · make a rooting bucket. Buy a one-gallon plastic paint bucket and fill the bottom with two and a half inches of small pebbles. Cover the pebbles with water. With a sharp knife, cut four one-inch horizontal slices in the bucket on a level with the top pebbles. Now fill the bucket with sand to within one inch of its top. Pour water over the sand until it starts to ooze through the slits. Let the bucket rest until all the superfluous water drains out and the sand is damp.

Each bucket will hold seven to ten cuttings. Do not use cuttings with flowers on them and use only the top six to eight inches of a stem. Strip the leaves from the bottom four inches of each stem and put them into a glass of water.

Use a pencil to make holes in the sand. Dip each stem one at a time into RooTone and insert it into a pencil hole. Snug sand around each stem with your finger. When the bucket is full, set it outdoors in a shady spot. After about ten days the cuttings should perk their heads up and look alive.

After thirty, days carefully dig up one cutting and check for a ball of roots. If the roots appear healthy, plant the cutting in the garden where you want it to bloom. If the roots do not look healthy, replant the cutting in the sand and return the bucket to the shade for another week.

Usually the bucket doesn't have to be watered after it's made up, but if the sand looks dry, add a little water.

DO· root roses in November. Root chrysanthemums and boxwood from new growth in early April. Root hydrangeas from new growth in June. Root oleander cuttings when they are in bloom. Put the cuttings in glass jars of water and put them in the shade outdoors. In six weeks they'll be ready to plant.

DO · winter over pots of your favorite impatiens in your house. On February 1 cut them back completely. In three weeks time they will have put out enough new growth to provide cuttings. Put these cuttings in water. They will be ready to plant in pots of dirt by March.

SEEDS

D O · plant sweet pea and larkspur seeds in November. Plant nasturtium seeds on Washington's birthday. Plant cosmos seeds about March 10.

STRAWBERRY JARS

D O · fill a strawberry jar with plants.

Buy an eighteen- or twenty-inch strawberry jar and plant in it one of the following:

> *Strawberry plants*
> *Pansies*
> *Violas*
> *Begonias*
> *Johnny-jump-ups*

Buy the small six-pack of these plants. Remember that their roots must fit through the openings in the jar.

To create the "plumbing" for the strawberry jar, take a sixteen-inch-long piece of two-inch plastic piping and put a plastic cap on one end (PVC is easily cut and glued). Bore four one-eighth-inch holes around the sides of the pipe starting one inch from the bottom and repeating every two inches up to the top. Fill the pipe with small pebbles and set it aside.

Now, the following procedure is important to the success of your project. The bottom of a strawberry jar has a drainage hole that must be carefully covered with small pieces of broken clay pots (these are called shards). There must be enough pieces to keep your soil from washing out yet they must be arranged so that no water backs up into the pot. The pot must drain! These shards are the seat upon which you will settle your plastic pipe and the pipe must sit level so that the water that's to be poured into it drains out evenly on all sides. Only the excess will drain out the bottom.

Place the pipe with the pebbles in it down into the jar and balance it on the shards. Cover the top of the pipe with tinfoil, then pour enough potting soil, into the jar to reach the first level of openings. Put one plant into each opening. Now add more potting soil, covering the roots of the first plants and reaching to the next level of openings. Gently water the soil at this point. The soil will settle and a bit more will have to be added. Put in your next circle of plants and follow the same procedure until you reach the top of the jar. Take the tinfoil off the pipe and fill the pipe to overflowing with water. The water level in the pipe will decline as the water seeps into the soil through the holes you made, watering the plants along the way. When it's time to fertilize, put liquid fertilizer in the pipe. Place the jars up on bricks so the excess water can drain away.

Strawberry jars make a pretty addition to any patio space and can serve as a focal point in a small area or as an ornament by an entrance.

CAMELLIAS

D O · buy camellias when they are in bloom. That's the only way to be sure you get your heart's desire. When buying camellias, notice the growth pattern of their leaves—the shape of the leaf and how it grows on the bush. A camellia will bloom only for a month to six weeks, but that handsome foliage is with you year-round.

D O N ' T · plant camellias in full sun. After a frosty night, the rays of the morning sun will ruin a bloom. Also, too much sun turns the leaves a sickly yellowish green. Plant camellias in shady areas about an inch above the surrounding ground level to assure good drainage.

In late September, sprinkle two cups of dehydrated cow manure around each plant. This provides food for the improved blooms in December, January, and February. At the same time, treat some of the buds on each camellia with a drop of gibberellic acid. To do this, break off a bud and put a drop of gibberellic acid into the little cup formed by the break. Then wait patiently for the delightful results. The next bloom will be early and considerably larger.

In February, fertilize your camellias with one of the commercially prepared camellia fertilizers.

In April, paint the first eighteen inches of each stalk with Cygon. This keeps the plants free of the white film that often forms on the backs of leaves.

Prune the inner branches and twigs to assure good air circulation and pick up the fallen blooms on a daily basis.

AZALEAS

DO · use azaleas, which are dense and evergreen, for boundary planting. Buy them when in bloom to be certain of getting the colors and varieties you want. Fertilize azaleas just after they bloom and prune them at the same time. You may need to prune them again in early June. Like camellias, they need some shade and should be planted slightly above ground level to assure good drainage.

Give extra care to color selection, for azaleas are highly colored and have a large mass of blooms. Their beauty can be enhanced by planting solid evergreens among them. The use of white azaleas planted among the colored ones also helps to defuse that sense of being overwhelmed. Handle azaleas wisely.

Spray azaleas with benomyl for petal blight just as their buds begin to show color and again in four days and still once more. This pays off. If you don't do it, you can find a bush that has just burst into bloom wilting within hours, and instead of dramatic beauty you have disaster.

ROSES

D O · plant roses! There are many good reasons to do so:

1. They are the ultimate horticultural treat. They are elegant.

2. This collector's dream comes in a wide variety of colors, shapes, sizes, and fragrances.

3. Cultivating roses is a challenge. You will worry about weather, location, soil, drainage, insects, and disease, but don't be deterred. It's like owning a thoroughbred Arabian horse. It can be an endeavor as complicated as a lawsuit involving a risk-taking but talented tax attorney and the Internal Revenue Service. But anything that adds excitement—intensity—to life should be welcomed with open arms.

Dr. Fletcher Derrick has been successfully growing roses in downtown Charleston for the last twenty-five years. He has generously suggested the following basic requirements:

- *Six to eight hours of sunlight daily*

- *Good drainage*

- *Two or three gallons of water per bush
per week and in the very hot months (if dry)
a gallon of water per bush per day.*

- *Year-round mulching*

- *Regular monthly feedings*

- *Regular spraying with a rose fungicide
once a week from April to November*

EXPERIMENTATION

DO · experiment. Looking back at these pages I realize there are many plants I've barely mentioned or haven't mentioned at all. Last year we sowed poppies at Miss Em's Yeaman's Hall garden. Bright yellow poppies, delicate and exquisite. And English daisies—I'm mixing them in pots this year with sweet alyssum. Queen Anne's lace is all over the mountainsides. It's a member of the carrot family. It should grow in my garden but I've never tried it. Shrimp plant is an old Charleston favorite I've neglected. It takes up so much room and blooms in the summer when I'm not here. Rose of Sharon, zinnias, sunflowers, and so many others don't find a home in my garden either because they're summer bloomers. But don't let that stop *you.*

CUTTING FLOWERS FOR THE HOUSE

DON'T · worry about sugar water or vinegar or this, that, and the other. Warm water will do in your vases, bowls, and other containers. And when you're about to decorate with something that doesn't look like a fresh daisy, stop and throw it away. It's plain-down common sense: Don't cut a flower that is almost finished and expect it to last a week in a container.

DO · gather flowers in the early morning, before the dew drys, or in the late afternoon. Each flower should be in half bud or just on the verge of opening fully. No amount of conditioning is going to help keep a flower fresh if it's already going downhill.

Remember, no foliage should be allowed under the waterline of an arrangement. It will quickly decay and produce an unpleasant smell.

As each flower is cut (using sharp clippers), submerge the stem deep into a container of warm water. Once you return to the house, recut each stem on the diagonal with a sharp knife underwater. This prevents air bubbles from getting into the stem and blocking the water from rising up the stem to the leaves and flower. Also, the diagonal cut opens a wider surface for the water to rise through and will not sit flat on the bottom of a container and seal itself. Now put this container in a dimly lit area and allow the stems to soak up water for three or four hours. After this treatment, the flowers will be ready to arrange and will last several days longer.

PARTING WORDS

D O · enjoy your garden. Play it by ear.